Notes on Loss

Notes on Loss

BY ALAN MITCHELL

THE CHOIR PRESS

Copyright © 2025 Alan Mitchell

All rights reserved. No part of this publication may be reproduced or transmitted in any form or by any means, electronic or mechanical including photocopying, recording or any information storage or retrieval system, without prior permission in writing from the publishers.

The right of Alan Mitchell to be identified as the authors of this work has been asserted by him in accordance with the Copyright, Designs and Patents Act 1988

First published in the United Kingdom in 2025 by

The Choir Press

ISBN 978-1-78963-556-0

For Christine

Author's Note

Worlds of experience are lost in silence, but it doesn't have to be that way. Our lives are a story about what we have gained and lost and how we deal with mortality. Most of us internalise loss and suffer in silence, when the catharsis of articulating our feelings might help us and point the way for others to follow.

Introduction

There is only one guarantee in life and that is we are all going to die. Frequently, the prelude to our own death is to witness the death of someone we love, but we continue to live life as if we were immortal. Even when we watch someone we love die we do not believe that will also be our fate. The collision of life (and its tapestry of illusions) with death strikes us with grief – a state where life's illusions are replaced with emotional emptiness stretching to the edge of sanity. *Notes on Loss* recounts my faltering route through the desolation I endured following my partner, Christine's, death.

Perhaps the best way to describe the structure of *Notes on Loss* is to imagine a piece of glass depicting the life I shared with Christine and that her death shattered the glass into countless fragments, some of which entered my mind and I wrote down. Inevitably, many fragments are missing but I hope those that follow contain both an individual and interrelated coherence that provides an insight into my reason for writing Notes on Loss.

Thoughts

Awake or asleep there are always thoughts. Diversion is undermined by thoughts. Mechanical actions submit to thoughts. The action is there, but the thoughts are here, inside, at my core. Sleep's oblivion works for a while. Then the chaotic thoughts, called dreams, intrude. Then I awake and the chaotic and cruel thoughts of consciousness resume. Fragments of you in my thoughts, in my dreams. Thoughts have no weight, but they weigh me down. I have the rock of Sisyphus embedded in my stomach, but unlike Sisyphus I cannot move it. There is no summit to reach, for temporary respite, no time for the comfort of reflection, as the rock rolls away. There is only the drag of the weight of my thoughts and the emotional exhaustion it engenders.

The garden

I walk around the garden, but the solace I expect to find is gone. There are signs of life, of rebirth, but you won't see them. I long for spring, but that will take me further from you. "April is the cruellest month" will certainly be true and May and June and............?

I stopped to look at snowdrops. Then I cried. Tears are like my thoughts – I can't control them. I hope that someone will see me crying and comfort me. As long as I had you, I didn't need "someone", or anyone. Now, with you gone, my heart is a wound of emptiness, where I once had you. Will the wound ever heal? No, because I'll never have you. I created the garden for you – for your approval. You thought it was my obsession, but that was you. When you said how beautiful it was you fulfilled me. You were the confident one, while I was your uncertain, easily bruised "rough boy".

The house

This was our house, so you are everywhere. Everywhere I look, every step I take you follow me. My mood lifts, because I anticipate I'll find you, that you will arrive soon, but, of course, you won't. The illusion of your presence (a phantom created by loneliness) gives me hope and then reality dashes it.

I know you are dead. I watched you die. I saw the infinity of death in your eyes and the rapid transformation in your face, from Christine's face to a dead person's face – any dead person's face. I looked back, as I left your room in the hospice. That was a mistake. The final image of that mistake will always haunt me, because you can't unsee what has been seen. You never looked back. You were right.

Selfies

When you lose someone and you are in a state of shock memories lack coherence, but they do not lack cruelty, as they push their way to the forefront of your mind. Whether it was the euphoric effects of the drugs, or just seizing a few moments of desperate happiness, you decided to take some selfies. You were in Ward 41, where I think you thought there was some hope. Even though you couldn't eat solid food, you had a tube inserted through your nostril to drain your stomach and another tube draining your bladder, you still had the courage to defy what was killing you. A line from a Dostoevsky novel entered my mind, (while I watched you posing for your selfies), "I did not bow down to you, I bowed down to the suffering of all humanity."

My birthday

I'm 65 today. From the age of 29 to 64 you celebrated my birthdays with me. You, like most women, believed it was important to mark special days. Now, you are not here, there is nothing to celebrate. Now each day will run into the next until, like you, I too run out of days.

Keeping this diary

Sometimes I miss days in this diary, which is not in the strict sense a diary. Then I catch up with the days I've missed. What would you make of my sad efforts to maintain some kind of contact with you? You would probably chide me for not keeping up but forgive me because I didn't have the benefit of the discipline your early life inculcated in you. Was part of our relationship always that of teacher and errant, but quite promising pupil? If so, how can I be expected to maintain this sad document when my teacher has gone?

Death

I watched Christine die, but I am unable to comprehend what I saw, because my frame of reference was stopped by death. Life is knowable, but there is no way to know death. Nothing in life prepares you for death's finality, because nothing can.

We understand life and the living, but we cannot understand death, because it exists beyond life. The eyes of the living have been called the mirrors of the soul. The eyes of the dead should be called the mirrors of infinite emptiness. Years ago, I fatally injured an animal, which I carried to the side of the road where I watched life leave its eyes. There is no more profound change than that transition. One minute this creature was looking at me and then its eyes seemed to look beyond me to infinite emptiness.

The difference between the engagement of life and the disengagement of death is most profoundly reflected in the eyes. On the night before Christine's death her eyes were strangely luminous. They looked beyond me, then, briefly, they looked at me then they looked through me. The lack of recognition crippled me with grief. I looked down and cried, because, although you would not be dead until the next day, your eyes told me I had lost you. I wonder what you thought, looking at me and listening to me cry? I hope you didn't ask yourself, "who is that crying" and "why is he here?" But I was losing you to your pain and drug-induced confusion, so, although we had shared many moments of closeness and tenderness the last time you looked at me was through the eyes of a stranger.

The following day, you died three minutes before I arrived at the hospice. I thought, as I entered your room – we never said goodbye, but death did that for us. I sat with you for a long time. Your eyes were open, so I tried to close them. They would not close, so I thought what you see in films when the grief-stricken husband or wife gently closes the eyes of their partner is for dramatic effect, rather than reflecting reality. Subsequently, a nurse closed your eyes. I thought, in a disconnected way, she must know the technique. I looked at you and I felt profoundly sorry for you. You didn't deserve this. I suppose I was in a state of shock. I felt I should get up and discuss what happens now with the nurse, but I had no energy. The offer of a cup of tea rescued me from the trance-like limbo of not thinking and doing nothing. The nurse said I could collect your things the next day, but I saw no reason to come back, so the nurse and I bundled your belongings into a few black plastic bags. As I put these in the boot of the car, a line from an old song came to mind, "Is that all there is?" I returned to your room to check nothing had been left there, then as I turned to leave, I saw the Snowdrops I had brought from our garden. They too were dead.

Christine's funeral

Perhaps it's a strange thing to say, but Christine would have approved of her funeral. She was a very well organised person. Every detail had to be right, or it was wrong. There was no compromise. And, given my emotional state, I wasn't sure the details of the funeral would work, but they did. You liked people, so you would have approved of the large gathering at the service and then afterwards at the hotel. The Celebrant I contacted had been a colleague and I knew you liked him, so I thought you would have approved of my choice. I managed to hold it together while recounting details of your life before and after we met, even when I quoted the words from your last Christmas card, "Hoping for better days" and then concluding, sadly, that the better days never came. However, when your son quoted the words of an old song, "Thank you for the days, Those endless days, those sacred days you gave me", I couldn't stop the tears.

Poem from Christine's Order of service

A Memory

Many times I have held you
In satin soft moments of birth
When from sleep's womb we were thrust
Into the vortex of another busy day.

Our eyes closed, refusing to open,
We lived blind, like small creatures,
Advancing by sense of touch alone
Till the light insisted on wakefulness.

Then our eyes met and with a smile
Lips moved close to close on lips
Across the downy landscape.

Alan.

"Immortal mortals, mortal immortals, living their death and dying their life" Heraclitus (born 6th century BC)

We live life as if we won't die. Even when we watch someone, we love die we do not believe that will also be our fate. That is why, fundamentally, life is an illusion and death is the only reality.

Ardgour

I collected Christine's ashes today, so why don't I believe she is dead and will never come back? When spring comes, I will drive to Glencoe and bury her ashes beside those of her parents, so she can marvel for eternity at the view across Loch Leven to the rugged hills of Ardgour. It was a beautiful day when we buried her parents' ashes. I remember we sat very still and said nothing. This time, I will sit alone. I have it in mind to prepare a place for my ashes next to Christine's, but I'm certain I will only ever look to the hills of Ardgour in life, not in death.

Grief

Grief doesn't die until the grieving person dies.

Silence

Silence used to be my friend, but now it is my brooding enemy.

Time

"Sometimes I want to murder time, sometimes when my heart's aching ......". Time is the most unforgiving of human inventions. We fear its passing, because we can't control it. We sense the hourglass of our life emptying, so we rush to the receding future, when living in each moment would make more sense. While every passing minute is sixty seconds long, that is seldom how we experience it. Time can drag, can perversely lead you to want it to speed up – to fill the void that, in its pitiless emptiness, is crushing you. "Time heals everything" is comforting, but untrue. The passage of time might lead to forgetting, but that is not healing. We were together for thirty-six years and there was never enough time, so we made the most of every minute. Time was our ally, because we thought we controlled it. Then time was our enemy, because we were under its control, as it led us, inexorably, through your decline and to your death. But while death ended time for you, time continued, relentlessly, for me.

Hillwalking

I climbed Ben Vorlich today. The weather was perfect. The conditions – winter sun, blue skies, deep snow, transformed this minor Munro into a minor Alp. The clarity of everything was astonishing. The sun, above the seemingly endless panorama of snow-covered hills, the white of which appeared to be suffused with the flawless blue sky, was like a starburst above me and a reflection of molten gold on the surface of the loch below me. The summit trig point was a weathered work of art, plastered with wind blasted roughly encrusted snow, which looked like poorly applied icing on a bizarre cake.

I felt alive – the brightness, the biting wind, the sharply defined images, fed my need for an escape from cruel memories, depression and death.

I loved you and I still love you, but, after the darkness of your death, I'm drawn to the light. To the knife-edged contours on the snow, to the snow that is so white, it seems blue.

Contrast and contradiction create confusion in life.

Enjoying the sun

The weather has been lovely lately, sunny days and sunny evenings. I can remember, last summer, you sitting next to me holding a glass of white wine in your hand, while Sandy lay next to you and baked in her fur coat. You were kind to Star then. You would say it was like being on holiday, somewhere in rural France. This summer, what I have just described is a final memory, as both you and Sandy have gone. Now, when I sit in the sun I'm alone (except for the ghosts beside me), so I don't sit in the sun very often.

The right balance

A good friend came round for a coffee today. She is a precious resource, so I must be careful not to exhaust her. I want her company, but I do not deserve to want it too much. I must strike a balance whereby she doesn't feel I'm using her when there is nobody else or feel I'm over-using her by demanding too much of her company.

Dad

We meet in a pub. Christine's cruel death and my devastation aren't mentioned. Old people are immeasurably more selfish than children, because they know better.

Walking

I went for a long walk with a friend, who died in a tragic accident two years after I lost Christine. We spoke about you a lot, which was helpful. We set a fast pace, which had a cathartic effect, as the concerted purpose in the physical exercise helped banish the doldrums, which come with inaction. As Joseph Conrad said, "Action is consolatory. It is the enemy of thought and the friend of flattering illusions." Consolatory illusions were what I needed then and would need for a long time.

Our local pub

I have been drinking in our local pub for over 40 years, that is, before I met Christine. We, I, Christine and our friends have spent many a convivial evening there, but now Christine is one of the many ghosts that drink in the bar. Sometimes, I think there are more ghosts drinking there than living customers. One night I'll join them.

Friends

I spent the night at the home of two close friends. The way they look at me and care for me reflects how damaged I must look to them. I don't have many friends, but I value the friends I have. Later, I met another friend for coffee. She was Christine's friend more than mine, but she seems to want to maintain contact. I have always styled myself as a loner, but I was always a counterfeit loner. A loner with a hedge against actual loneliness, called Christine. Christine was the friend who enabled me to claim I did not need friends. Now she is gone, so my charade is exposed, i.e. that I am a loner afraid of being alone.

Saturday

I spend the day alone. I divert myself with cleaning the house and washing clothes. I put on a CD. Everything is fine until the song, "You belong to me" and the line, "You don't have to prove to me you're beautiful to strangers". That's the trigger and I break down. An old memory of when we were both young and unsure brings back my raw insecurity and jealousy, which was needless, because you did belong to me and I belonged to you.

Why?

Fragments and images seep through the barrier I've erected to prevent me from slipping down the slope into the despair of trying to understand your last three weeks of life and my failure to do anything but watch you die.

False sanctuary

I'm sitting on a beach, it's darkening, it's warm and the only sound – soft and comforting – comes from the gentle ebb and flow of the waves. The waves follow a rhythm of quiet rush and quiet retreat. Now and then the retreat creates a minor disturbance – an almost imperceptible flicker – that is there and gone. Then the waves return to their normal rhythm – undisturbed – until the next flicker. I think this occasional disturbance, this tiny movement to the rhythm of the waves is like someone's death. We, like the conditioned waves, console ourselves with the false sanctuary of routine and the delusion of immortality. We ebb and flow our way through life, quietly, purposefully, until the flicker of death disturbs us – permanently – and our relatives and friends – temporarily – until their respective tiny movements/deaths briefly distorts the rhythm of their lives and so on and on …

Sandy

You loved cats. Always cats, never dogs. Sandy left me before you. It was late December. Life had finished with Sandy and it was a cruel thing to see her drag herself across the kitchen floor, so I took her to the Vet, to ask for her to be released from her misery. Sandy looked at me, as the Vet injected her. The transition in her eyes from connection to disconnection (from life to death) was almost instantaneous. Later, in the car, I cried for Sandy, for me and, in anticipation of the inevitable, for you – for whom the compassion shown for Sandy was not possible.

Zola

In my late teens, long before I met you, I read some of the novels of the French writer Emile Zola. This was a time in my life when I was reading books about the struggles of the Working Class, a subject I empathised and identified with. The first Zola novel I read was "Germinal", which is the story of a coalminers' strike, in northern France. Germinal and the other Zola novels I read are part of the Rougon Macquart series, which comprise twenty novels set in the 19th century. The series focuses on the two branches of a family, the respectable Rougons and the disreputable Macquarts – over five generations. Zola believed in environmental and hereditary influences, which he explores through his characters in relation to, for example, violence, alcoholism and prostitution. It would be fair to say that Zola's novels present a pessimistic view of humanity, i.e. there are no happy endings. Several of Zola's novels have been made into films, including Germinal. When I met Christine, approximately ten years after reading Zola's novels, one of the things we discussed were the books we had read. I think the fact that my taste was more eclectic than hers, from "The Voyage of the Beagle", by Charles Darwin, to "The Jungle", by Upton Sinclair, intrigued Christine, given that I was poorly educated by comparison with her. I took it as a compliment when she started to read some of the books I recommended, including the novels of Emile Zola. Over the years, while we were together, we also enjoyed Zola novels which had been adapted for film or television, e.g. "Nana", "La Bete humaine" and "Therese Raquin".

Then time passed and we forgot about Zola until, years later, Christine became ill, whereupon she said she would like to finish reading the Rougon Macquart series of Zola's novels. I never questioned her reason for wishing to undertake this somewhat daunting task, instead I helped her to gather most of the novels in the series, which she did not possess. Ultimately, she obtained and read the twenty novels in the Rougon Macquart series, some in French because an English translation was not available. The worlds Zola creates in his novels are always vivid and frequently unrelenting. His male characters can be violent and his female characters are frequently abused and in consequence brooding and resentful. Life is a constant struggle against unforeseen circumstances that threaten to overwhelm those involved. I have asked myself why Christine wanted to immerse her thoughts in such a bleak and unremitting world. If it was to escape from the terminal illness that was killing her it was a strange choice.

Christine's choice

Christine chose to talk about life, not her death. I've heard that some people who are dying choose to talk about their death and even make plans for it. For what it's worth, I think Christine made the right choice. If talking about our death is the right thing to do, why don't we talk about death during every day of our lives, because we know we are going to die? Why hide behind the false sanctuary of comforting habits and routines until some medic pronounces your death sentence? How do you talk – meaningfully – about your death, as death is ultimately unknowable? You can talk about accepting your death (as if you have a choice in the matter!) and the practicalities, like funeral arrangements and your will, but that's just, somewhat morbid, final housekeeping. Christine knew she was dying, so her logic was, "why should I want to talk about it? Instead, she chose to ignore death by talking about the concerns of life and the living. That's why she was brave, much loved and admired.

The night before you died

I sat beside your hospice bed for several hours. You were obviously in considerable discomfort. Looking at you more closely, as I asked you about your pain, I noticed that your eyelids were stuck together with matter, so I dampened some tissues and cleaned them. Although the nurse should have done this, I felt grateful for her neglect, as it allowed me to overcome the barrier of the bed and show you some care and tenderness. I took great care with you. Perhaps I had a premonition that this was the last time I would touch you while you were alive. With your eyes clear, you looked around you. You seemed to look more into the middle distance, as if there was something there that was drawing your attention. Then you looked at me and I was crucified. Whatever you had done to deserve this end must have been a great sin indeed.

The supplicant who petitions humbly

When the sun shines I am accompanied by my shadow. My shadow can be comforting, a known companion. It can also be disconcerting, a black void with my outline – a mirror of my death. Across the threshold there are no shadows, but there is your presence and deafening silence. I seem to watch myself, as I walk from room to room and then fall to my knees while tears tear at my sanity. My arms are outstretched and my hands face upwards. I say "please" to no one. I am the supplicant who petitions humbly for respite that cannot be given.

"While you see a chance take it"
(Steve Winwood)

We are all selfish. When we do something for each other we seem to sublimate our selfishness. But the motivation, despite a mutually beneficial result, is always selfish. However, my selfishness over your selfishness (and vice versa) is cancelled out in mutual selflessness. It might seem to be a cold and cynical conclusion, but perhaps this somewhat ambivalent exchange is essential in a successful and loving relationship. Before we met, we were in relationships where our respective partners thought we were selfish, because we were unhappy and did not love them. (It is ironic that people who call other people selfish never consider that they are also selfish). There was no recognition that love is an exchange based on each partner giving, so each can take. The best love making exemplifies this selfless exchange. When we met and combined our selfish desires, we achieved something selfless in a love that lasted for over three decades.

Follow your emanation, but beware of the perilousness of action
(William Blake)

A long time ago we were raised to believe love (romantic love) was more than an attraction based on sexual desire, which the Christian religion condemns as lust. "After intercourse the animal is sad", is pure religious propaganda, as the "animal" (lustful human) cannot be anything but "sad" after indulging in the sinful activity of "intercourse". It goes without saying, for Christians, that sexual desire is selfish and outside of marriage wrong. However, describing an act as right or wrong is to deal in moral absolutes, when our actions are almost always morally contingent. In essence, we tailor our morality to suit our selfish needs and then, if we are Christians (of the Roman Catholic persuasion, for instance) we confess our moral perfidy, gain absolution and expect to sin again, because God's design flaw, otherwise known as human frailty, puts acting morally (in an absolute sense) beyond our capabilities. Measured against Christian values, we transgressed, because we followed our emanations. We were married and had children and we ignored the perilousness of our actions. We were driven together by forces that disappeared when we held each other. We were fugitives from a hypocritical morality we did not believe in, although we were not immoral. We escaped into an intimacy, which was innocent in its urgency, its passion and its tenderness. After intercourse we were never "sad", because we had given and taken equally, as lovers should. Rather than feeling immoral, we felt complete. We had the good fortune to be intellectually and physically compatible and rather than finding that sinful it gave us happiness, until chance (the ultimate arbiter) killed half of something that was beautiful and left the other half to grieve.

Music

There is more music in the house now, as I need the company. Music and lyrics have always had a profound effect on me. Although the artist is singing about their world and their experiences, I quickly identify with them and absorb them and they affect me, as if I had actually experienced the hurt or the happiness contained in the song. "All I want" is a Joni Mitchell song, but I have identified with it – totally – for much of my adult life. It's a song about longing, love and desire. When you are young, love and desire frequently merge. Physical need blurs with emotional dependency and the result is an insatiable driven innocence that is all-consuming. Before I met you, I identified with Joni when she sang, "Alive, alive I want to get up and jive, want to wreck my stockings in some juke box dive" and "Applause, applause life is our cause, when I think of your kisses my mind seesaws." After we met, we became lovers compelled by the urgency of the love and delirium of desire celebrated in "All I want", but with this difference, we were real and we were living it!

Keeping busy.

Housework, making changes, doing – not thinking – is a charade, not a release. Internal pressure parallels each positive act, which saps resolve. You must not give up, but your grief asks -" why not?"

Crying while driving

A Paloma Faith song triggers my tears. "Just Be" was playing, as I drove home. "Don't say nothing, just sit next to me. Don't say nothing, just be, just be, just be." Before the tears, I think back to last September and the two of us sitting in the sunshine beside Loch Faskally. We watched the ducks disturb the mirror image on the surface of the Loch and then the image repair itself, but we said nothing, having decided to "just be". Many times, we have sat next to each other and said nothing and in so doing achieved a closeness that transcended words. Where will I find that closeness now, I ask myself, as my tears obscure the dark road ahead?

Extract from a letter to a friend

Each day adds an extra day's distance from when Christine died, but she is still with me every waking hour of every day. Our culture has taught us to view History as a linear progression, while other cultures, especially the wise ancient ones, view it as being cyclical, i.e. a series of recurring events. According to linear progression, I should be travelling a line in time that distances me from losing Christine, but I'm not. My thoughts are dominated by the recurring events of my memories of our life together. I write these thoughts and memories down in a diary, which is not chronological, although it is dated. What determines what I write is what thoughts or memories are dominating my mind at the time? The fact that it is written on Thursday 15th May, for instance, is irrelevant, as there is no intrinsic connection between the date and what is written. Hence, the diary is more of a document of memories, thoughts, impressions and questions than a consecutive record of daily events. It is a double-edged sword, in that it maintains my contact with Christine, while making me feel lost at her loss. When you lose someone, you loved, you are like someone who is stumbling through unknown territory trying to find the way back to the comfort of the known. As that "someone", I think the best I can hope for is to occasionally glimpse "the comfort of the known", but I know it will always be on a horizon I can't quite reach.

Wherever you are you are here

I have climbed hills and mountains for most of my life. You thought it was an obsession and missed me when I was gone. And I missed you with every step of the way. Perversely, I seemed to leave you to think about you and to want you.

There is a time of day when the sun magnifies the beauty of hills and mountains with a sad mellowness. The sun retains its warmth but loses its glare. The day is coming to an end and the sun signals it is resigned to this by imbuing every colour with softness and sadness. I walk down the path feeling tired. I feel comfort in the silence that surrounds me. I think about what it is that keeps us together, while feeling the loss of us being apart. Impatient to see you and hold you, I console myself with this thought – wherever you are you are here.

"Pandora and the Flying Dutchman"

"According to the legend, the Flying Dutchman was condemned to wander the seas eternally unless he could find a woman who loved him enough to die for him." (That woman was Pandora). This quote describes the plot of an old film I watched recently. Logically, the film could not be taken seriously, but as a story about jealousy, guilt and the quest for unconditional love and salvation it enthralled me. In my mind – blurred with alcohol – I was Hendrik van der Zee (the Flying Dutchman) and you were Pandora, but in our story you had died too soon and left me to cling to the shipwreck of my desolation. If only I could believe we will meet again to bring us our salvation, but, in the sober light of day, that was a film and this is life and my only salvation will be my lonely death and the forgetfulness that follows.

Finding meaning in suffering (1)

"To live is to suffer, to survive is to find some meaning in the suffering" (Friedrich Nietzsche). As a theoretical statement that is easy to understand, but as a practical proposition finding meaning in suffering, especially the suffering of someone you love, is probably impossible to achieve. To find meaning in Christine's suffering, I would have had to divide myself into an objective self (looking for meaning in the suffering) and a subjective self, whose purpose was to support the person they loved, as she faced the last few weeks of a terminal illness, the pain, the inexorable deterioration and death in a hospice bed. As I loved Christine, I failed to achieve the required detachment, so I found no meaning in Christine's suffering, but, for what it's worth and despite that, I have survived.

Finding meaning in suffering (2)

When you share your life with someone you are always sharing the meaning of your life, because their integral involvement with you, emotionally, physically, intellectually, reciprocally, underpins the meaning of your life. When that underpinning is removed, through their death, a significant and irreplaceable part of your life's meaning is amputated. It is that brutal! As an emotional amputee you suffer, because so much meaning in your life has been removed. Like a man who has lost his legs, but still feels their presence, you refuse to believe in the finality of your loss. The question is, when will I accept what, logically, cannot be rejected.? How can I achieve that acceptance? I want to survive, but I cannot find any meaning in our suffering.

"Having the courage to suffer"

I quoted the heading (above) from somewhere, but I can't remember where. It's one of those statements that sounds defiant and in control, which for someone like Christine, who had terminal cancer, was both ridiculous and unjust. The inference seems to be that there is a choice, for people who suffer, between having the courage to bear their suffering, or not. What do you do if you don't have the courage to suffer? Suffering is not optional. In the case of cancer, it is an insidious and progressively painful part of the process that, frequently, ends in death. Christine was the most courageous person I have known, but she would never have claimed that she had the courage to suffer.

Life is the journey, time is the road

Loneliness is where you are and from where you want to continue Life's journey to some kind of happiness, but where departure is uncertain. Your need to depart being the only imperative, you hope to leave loneliness soon, while being aware that "soon" might never arrive. Loneliness, therefore, is the place you need to depart from, long to depart from, but you are in a nightmare where there are no departure signs and ever- diminishing time is the road, so all you can do is wait and hope.

The persistence of memory

If I had put this heading in inverted commas, it is likely that it would have referred to a painting by Salvador Dali. A painting of a dreamscape with melting watches. However, with no inverted commas I have the freedom to consider the persistence of memory from a more personal perspective. Christine's watch sits on the top of her chest of drawers. I placed it there when I brought back her clothes and other possessions from the hospice, after she had died. If I moved the watch, the persistence of memory would enable me to still see it there, but it is constancy I need – even if it is an illusion. I want the watch to lie there, exactly where I placed it, so that I do not have to search for it in the jumble of my mind, which would be the case were I to move it. I can also touch it and through some alchemy touch Christine.

The meaning of life

I was in a pub, writing about losing you, when some wag asked me if I was writing about the meaning of life. My answer was, "not really". However, perhaps, I thought, this age-old perplexity should be dealt with. The meaning of life, in my view, inheres in the fact that you are alive – end of! As for death, it has no meaning, because death is beyond life – hence it is beyond meaning.

The solace of drink

After you died, I drank, but, surprisingly, not to excess. I stood on the edge of the abyss of alcohol, more than once, but then I stepped back. I don't really know why, because what would the Scottish character be without the solace of drink? If the Scots are melancholy with drink, what would they be without it? They would be a Nation of suicides!

Taxonomy and other illusions

I know for certain that there is life, because I am living it and there is death, because I have witnessed it. These are the two realities, the two non-contingent truths – everything else – including Taxonomy – is speculation. The evidence for this assertion is that the "speculation" changes frequently, to more, or less, or different speculation. However, the constant is that it is all speculation, except for the bare facts of life and death.

North Berwick

You once said that although you could remember what your parents looked like, you couldn't remember, clearly, what they sounded like. I suppose, therefore, I'm lucky, because over the years my interest in photography led me to make short videos, some of which include you. One such video was taken at North Berwick. I was trying out my latest video camera and you, Mum, Dad and my younger daughter were my willing – or at least patient – subjects. I decided on the spur of the moment to introduce myself as someone who was making a documentary about why tourists visited North Berwick. Although you knew I was acting the fool, you were all prepared to play along with me. The facile nature of the questions I asked, in a mock posh Scottish accent, elicited answers which caused everyone to laugh. I have looked at that piece of film often and thought how priceless it is to me. An event caught a long time ago, but available when I need to hear your voice and see you happy and healthy and sounding quite like Jean Brodie – in her prime!

Laughter

I like to laugh, to keep things light, because my core perspective is bleak. I like to laugh, because of my working-class origins. The working-class don't have much, so they console themselves with laughter. Christine, because of her middle-class origins, took life more seriously and only laughed at a prescribed list of things. I laugh at what I find funny, not at what is appropriately funny. I accept that humour is cruel, whereas Christine thought it shouldn't be. Had she lived, Christine would have been sympathetic to Snowflakes. If this sounds like a criticism it's not, as I found Christine's habit of explaining a joke to me, which I had already laughed at and drawn to her attention, both funny and very endearing.

Where education fails

There are no courses or qualifications that prepare you for dying or grieving.

The purpose of life

What the hell else is there in life but living it!

Christine's birthday

The day reflects the sadness of remembering your birthday. The sky is crying for you, from a countenance of grey. I searched for my last birthday card to you but couldn't find it. But I found a "Thank You" card from you, in which you wrote the following:

"To Alan,

- Who has borne all my burdens with me
- Whose life I have changed irrevocably
- Who has done his and my share of the chores without complaint

I can only hope that in the very near future something like normality may be achieved for both of us.

From Christine, with love and gratitude."

"Hope is the last thing to die", so I read somewhere, but hope is difficult to find when you lose someone who was half of your world.

Star

In the 18th and 19th centuries the village of Star was comprised of linen weavers' cottages, which were built to support the flax growing and linen weaving industry in Fife. Although, by the time we moved to Star, in the early 1980s, the weaving industry had long gone, the Primary School, dating from 1816 (a year after the Battle of Waterloo) was still educating village children. Star, despite its rural obscurity, had a novel written about it called, "The Gates of Eden", which was published in 1893. Annie S. Swan (the author) and her husband moved to Star, from Edinburgh, so he could teach at the Primary School. As they left Star, after two years, it would suggest that moving from Edinburgh, to what was then a very small village, was too much of a culture shock.

We moved to Star (and lived there for over 30 years), principally because I wanted a large garden. Edinburgh was our hometown and prior to moving to Star we had lived in another smaller town, but I was drawn to the large virtually empty green space that I longed to transform into an attractive garden, the open spaces around Star and the views of the Lomond Hills from our lounge window. Your attitude to living in Star was, to begin with quite ambivalent, but as we were only two miles away from the main railway line connecting Markinch to Edinburgh this tempered your uncertainty. However, you did resent the many hours I spent transforming the garden from part of a boggy field (hence the house name, Hallfield) to a suitable environment for ornamental trees, flowering shrubs and perennials such as:

Hellebores, Primulas, Iris, Meconopsis and my obsession, species lilies.

If the garden was my domain, the house was yours. I would help in the house, but always under your guidance. Visitors commented on the amount of light in the house and how, wherever they were, they found themselves looking through a window into the garden. Gradually, your ambivalence about the garden changed, although you continued to feel I gave it too much. We both loved the month of May, because the sun imbued the leaves on the trees and the flowers on the shrubs with a vibrancy that seemed to make them pulse with new life. Warm days released delicate natural perfumes from Daphnes, Azaleas and Rhododendrons. We described a yellow Azalea, with a sweet perfume, not unlike Honeysuckle, as "the scent of May". On warm evenings the scent would drift through our open patio doors and into our lounge to remind us of the glorious day we had spent together in the garden. However, the most singular perfume came from a tall Rhododendron, with pink buds and dozens of trusses of large white flowers. The perfume from the flowers seemed to scent the air in concentric circles, which became more intense the closer you got to the flowers. We both found it impossible to adequately describe this scent, because its effect was totally sensory and therefore beyond words.

In summer you seemed to forget you had reservations about living in Star. When the weather was fine, we ate breakfast beside a bed of Azaleas, enjoying the different colours and the delicate scent, while facing east to catch the rays of the morning sun. Then, after working in the garden all day, we ate our evening meal on the patio, facing west, lingering over a glass or two of wine until the sun set, whereupon we moved indoors. That is when you were most complementary about living in Star, when you said it was like living in rural France – your favourite country. Days like these were days of simple shared enjoyment. They were not unusual, but they deserved to be remembered, as their worth had no equivalent in the world of materialism. Our answer to the question about whether it was more important to have material things or to experience life (to have or to be) was exemplified through the way we developed and enjoyed our garden, over many years.

After you died, I kept out of the garden for a long time, because the loneliness seemed worse than the loneliness I felt in the house, as I walked past the plants we knew so well and discussed so often. However, as winter developed into spring, my desire to become part of the annual rebirth was strong enough to pull me back into the "magic garden", as I called it. But things would never be the same without you by my side.

Hogmanay

We kissed and embraced to welcome in the New Year. Then we separated and you looked into my eyes. It was a heartbreaking look, which seemed to say, "I'll be gone soon, so this will be our last embrace to welcome in a New Year together." My response to the defeat in your eyes and the sadness of our tragedy, which had less than a month to run its course, was to hold you until you felt the time was right to move away.

Silence

Nietzsche said something like – man can't take too much reality – and my recent experience of losing you exemplifies that he is right. I try to keep busy. Joseph Conrad said: "Action is consolatory. It is the enemy of thought and the friend of flattering illusion". But I need the consolation to be found in action and thought *is* my enemy and what I would give for some flattering illusions to rescue me from my despair. I play music – loudly. I drive about. I climb hills. I wander about the garden. I email people. I do this, that and the next thing, but there are still times when silence stalks me and then corners me. Silence seems to be more than an absence of sound. If silence could be weighed, or its substance investigated, I'm sure it would be heavy and dense. However, as silence is, apparently, just an absence of sound, my impressions about its heaviness and denseness must only exist in my mind. When silence corners me it brings bad memories. The fragments of these memories cut me with their unforgiving sharpness. I see you in various stages of decline. I see myself as a caring automaton, visiting you in the hospice and refusing to face what was happening to you, because I am a man and I can't take too much reality.

The search for meaning

"And this is how it is: if only you do not try to utter what is unutterable then nothing gets lost. But the unutterable will be – unutterably – contained in what has been uttered!" (Ludwig Wittgenstein)

Searching for meaning is a need that is natural to human beings. Human beings want to know why things happen. This is especially true when we lose someone. We feel compelled to make sense of why someone we loved suffered and died. This compulsion dominates and torments our thoughts. We have memories (usually fractured by our experience), thoughts and spoken and written language, to help us in our quest for meaning and to help us articulate what happened and why. We could simply say, "She had terminal cancer, which did not respond to treatment, so she died." But that is "what happened", not "why". Comments like: **"There is almost no consensus about what constitutes meaning. We possess the concept, but we don't know what to say about it" (Colin McGinn),** are less than helpful, but they may be true. Perhaps, it is not only that we don't know what to say about it, but that we don't have the words with which to say it. When faced with defining meaning, spoken and written communication are inadequate, because we are not sure what we mean by "meaning". This inadequacy is at its most profound when we are dealing with a personal tragedy. What we see and hear, as we watch and listen to the person we love dying, might give greater access to meaning, i.e. the why of the whole experience (assuming there is a "why"), but it is essentially "unutterable", so it is confounded, when words are used to convey the meaning of what we have seen or heard. We leave the hospice room with a mind full of cruel images: the tubes draining the waste from a shattered body; the greyness of mottled limbs; the drug-induced lightness of the grip on life, being a witness to ugliness when one remembers beauty. A belief in God could give meaning to suffering, in that death could lead to entry to heaven and a blissful eternity. But, as Nietzsche wrote, **"If you want to achieve peace of mind and happiness, then have faith; if you want to be a disciple of truth, then search."** For those who do not have faith, who do not know what to believe, the alternative seems to be to search. But (as has already been stated) searching, in relation to what we mean by meaning is a dead end, made so by the limitations of language. **"Language is but a broken light on the depths of the unspoken" (Bertrand Russell).** Perhaps that is why meaning is beyond our reach and why, when someone we love dies, words fail us.

The only reality

The search for meaning
Is a meaningless quest
So sometimes we rest
Rest in the moment
These moments
Of brief elation
Confirm our only reality.

The solace of figurative language

It seems impossible to explain feelings without recourse to similes, metaphors, alliteration, personification, analogy and other impressionistic devices of language use. Perhaps that is because they enable us to support the burden of unvarnished reality.

The figment of normality

I am acting a part, but the reviewer of the performance (who is also the actor) is not convinced. I watched some Choughs in the Dolomites. They chattered around me, then slipped over the edge of the cliff. I wonder if, one day, I will follow the Choughs.

Epitaph

"I come down from the misty mountains, I got lost on the human highway." Neil Young wrote my epitaph years ago. Christine thought "misty mountains" were lonely, uncomfortable places. She liked people, because she needed them. She was, ultimately, frightened of the solitude I, naturally, seek. However, although the "human highway" repels me, I do value the company of a few friends, the most important of whom was Christine.

Death – Hollywood style

What do we expect from the dying? People said how easy Christine made visiting her, because she never mentioned the fact that she was dying. Her consultant spoke in terms of, "I wouldn't expect anything less from Christine", because she was very polite and didn't ask awkward questions. Hollywood is an illusion factory, where the reality of death becomes part of the fantasy. I think Hollywood would have applauded Christine's way of dying, as it had the requisite style. Perhaps I should have asked Christine more questions regarding how she really felt about what was happening to her. Instead of which, I played the role she assigned to me, a) because that is what she wanted, b) because I did not feel I had the right to do other than fulfil her wishes and c) because I loved her.

"I am on a lonely road and I am travelling."

(Joni Mitchell)

I'm on a train heading south to visit my daughters. The train is full of very loud football supporters until it reaches Newcastle. However, I start to read "The Snow Leopard", by Peter Matthiessen (for the 4th or 5th time), so quickly leave the Tennent's lager swilling "raconteurs" to enter the world of ravines and towering, mountains in Nepal. Christine said my contempt for football and football supporters was a form of snobbery. I once wrote, "Herds, we all belong to one whether common or refined, touching arses for reassurance, as apes are so inclined." Hence, football isn't the problem, it's the "crowd mentality" that seems to require people to act like threatening, boorish idiots. If abhorring that kind of behaviour makes me a snob, then so be it!

"I think therefore I am"

(Rene Descartes)

"I" separates, so Buddhists seek to overcome the "I" – the awareness of self – to achieve an immersion in the freedom that lies beyond particular things. Every morning, we awaken to "I", to our own self-awareness, but to the Buddhist we are still asleep. Only when we "awaken" to the reality that the world of "particular things" is an illusion will we be not be asleep. Here and there, in "The Snow Leopard", the author, Peter Matthiessen, mentions his wife's death from cancer. Clearly, he felt guilty about the way he treated her. Then (at a Zen meeting) he achieves (through meditation) a state that imparts a kind of euphoria and sense of absolution, as far as his guilt, in relation to his wife, is concerned. A cynic might say, "How convenient". I never sought absolution, as far as my treatment of Christine was concerned. My guilt, from when I hurt her, is my punishment and so it should be. Perhaps, however, the way my love for Christine grew until the day she died brought a kind of absolution, but, hopefully, of a more honest and less esoteric kind.

God is dead and it's no big deal

Nietzsche may, or may not, have said "God is dead", but it was not an uncommon thought among the intelligentsia of his day. Now even ordinary people accept this famous/infamous quote, without giving it much thought. However, as the son of a clergyman and someone who was an unquestioning believer in his youth, Nietzsche's decision to live without God marked a huge existential change in his life. I wonder if Nietzsche ever really lost the comforting habit of relying on the existence of God. Was his self-image, as a 19th century German Zarathustra, not just the heroic posturing of someone who had really resurrected God in his heart of hearts? If Nietzsche deluded himself, Christine certainly didn't, as she faced her dying and her death without God and with a bravery that, I'm sure, Nietzsche would have thought admirable, but which is becoming more and more "no big deal" today.

Living in the present and thinking about the future

Christine did not have much time for reflection. The past was past, so what was the point of dwelling on it was her philosophy. I wonder if that was because some of the hurt and disappointments in her life were too raw to be analysed. When I first met her Christine was quite damaged. She had been hurt in a loveless marriage, so she thought my hopes for us demonstrated my lack of experience. I think she considered my love for her as naïve and almost childlike. It was only when she saw the steel behind my starry eyes that she became less cynical about our chances of having a future together. I'm not sure, however, that I was able to heal those early wounds. The song "Miss you nights" contains the line, "I've had many times I can tell you, times when innocence I'd trade for company", which, as a proud person, must have been hard for her to accept.

The invisible wall

The invisible wall is a metaphorical way of describing the most destructive barrier that can impact on relationships. It is built when love and trust have been lost. The invisible wall is built from alternate layers of misunderstanding and complacency, bonded together with resentment. Those who build the wall blame each other, which only helps to build the wall. Holding grudges and withholding forgiveness enhances the bitter skills of the builders of the invisible wall. Memories can breach the invisible wall, because they frequently recall the start of a relationship, rather than the sad present and the uncertain future. They recall a kiss in the sun, the passion, the need to and the escape from the complacency of predictable daily life. Unexpected acts of kindness can also breach the invisible wall. The longer the invisible wall stands, the more distance it creates between those who built it. It is a paradox, that something, which only exists in the minds of the builders, can create physical and emotional barriers that can destroy a once loving and caring relationship. The impulse of the builders seems to be, why create a little bit of heaven on earth when we can create a little bit of hell? There were times when Christine and I fought. Our arguments could be bitter and vicious, to such an extent that in the aftermath we felt emotionally and physically exhausted. In me, after we had argued, the storm passed quickly and the sun was out, so it was time to move on. For you, my transformation indicated that I hadn't meant what I had said, because I said it in anger. Our love for each other overcame the impulse to bear grudges and withhold forgiveness, so, despite our combative natures, we never built an invisible wall.

Edinburgh

Edinburgh was our home city and we both loved it. We loved the history, the architecture, the green open spaces, the culture, the ornately decorated public houses and the many and varied restaurants.

Although we grew up in Edinburgh, we didn't meet until we were working in the same College, which was situated in a small town north of Edinburgh. After we stopped looking for ways to "accidentally" meet in corridors and instead developed an intense relationship, you asked me if I would be prepared to become involved in a play the College Drama students were putting on in the Edinburgh Festival. The venue was the Traverse Theatre, which had a history that included a period when it was a brothel. Fortunately, the incarnation of the Traverse Theatre we performed in was less dubious. I say fortunately, because the subject of the play, we were about to perform, was biblical. As an avowed atheist, I had little interest in the plot of the play, but I was besotted with you, so I did what you asked. Initially, I was given one part to play, but ultimately, I had to deal with four parts.

My experience of the Theatre was as an audience member, not as a cast member, so I was in a constant state of trepidation about mixing up my parts and/or forgetting my lines. The fact that you and the Welsh director, who reminded me of Dylan Thomas with black hair, assured me I had nothing to worry about did not reassure me. However, your faith in me was not misplaced, as I didn't forget my lines and on one occasion frightened the pants off the audience, because I moved, very swiftly, from being very still and very silent to leaping towards centre stage while delivering my lines clearly and stridently.

After the performances were over, the cast made their way to the Festival Club, in Edinburgh High Street. I loved being with you there, because I felt relaxed and we benefitted from the anonymity of being a comfortable distance from where we lived. We were new to each other and we couldn't hide it. We sat and looked at each other, devouring each other with our eyes. We moved closer to each other and I put my arm around you. The heat from our bodies made us want each other, but that wasn't possible, so it was a sensual torture that had to wait to be satisfied.

My performance debut, at the Traverse Theatre, was also the end of my acting career, as I was never to tread the boards again. Within a few months we had moved in together, so you didn't need the diversion of the College Drama Group. However, we visited Edinburgh regularly, because our love of the city never died. Essentially, we were part of it and it was part of us. After your death, I continued to visit Edinburgh, but there was always something missing and of course that something was you.

Love

When two people meet, who are looking to be rescued from their respective lives, who have in the words of an old song a "Hungry Heart", do they sense the other person is the answer they have been looking for? Is there something in their respective body language and, especially, in the look in their eyes that tentatively nurtures the connection which might develop into love? Or is it just the influence of chance – like most things in life?

When we met, did we know we would fall in love and spend over thirty years together? To "fall in love", it sounds like you lose your balance and, emotionally, that is certainly true. It would be nice to say we did know, but it would also be dishonest, as initially we weren't sure of each other, but something caused us to persist until we made the commitment that, surprisingly quickly, became love.

In our experience, love started with physical and then emotional attachment. Shared interests, for example: nature, politics, books and music, strengthened our physical and emotional bond. However, we found love was more than a marriage of desirable things, it was first and foremost an expression of need – a need to escape loneliness and a need for fulfilment. It seems, there is a tension in love, between "a marriage of desirable things" and "need" – driven by the fear of loss – which commits each person to compromise for their love and, inevitably, this has a personal cost that can cause resentment. This "fear" both cements and undermines shared love. Its presence is always there, along with the ambivalent effect it can have. Physical, emotional and intellectual attraction are all positive aspects of love, but the undercurrent, of the fear of loss, can manifest itself as a negative force. However, its existence seems to be essential to hold love together, so this negative has a, paradoxically, positive effect. The following narrative, summarised from the many written words we exchanged, provides some idea of the interplay between the negative and positive forces that had an important bearing on our relationship and our love.

"People age, words don't"

Essentially, this is about how wonderful our love making was. My language is high flown and joyous. I am clearly totally besotted by the pleasure we give each other. What is fascinating is that the deliriously happy tone of the letter is as fresh as it was when I wrote it many years ago. I am getting old, but the words in the letter have remained as youthful as their author was all those years ago. People age, words don't.

"Clinging to the wreckage of each other"

The tone of the letter is driven by disappointment, anger and despair. You left a loveless, but financially comfortable marriage, so what we had together was not enough. You were better educated, more hardheaded and more worldly wise than I, whereas I was a young poorly educated man who, in my innocence, thought my love would be enough for you. This letter is from the time in our relationship when we almost broke up, but the prospect of going back to our old, emotionally desolate, lives made us cling to the wreckage of each other, in the hope that things would improve, which, fortunately, they did.

"Circumstance is a perverse bastard, a whimsical manipulating deviant deriving pleasure from the pain it inflicts on humanity"

A change of plan puts you beyond my reach, so I overreact.

"If I appear quiet and distant then wait, I'll return to you"

I wrote a potted autobiography of a working-class cliché, to give you some idea of how I had become who I was.

"My lover and my mentor"

A letter filled with my gratitude for the interest and support you give me. I don't think you ever realized how much I owed you. Your support enabled me to succeed in a way that would have been very difficult without your belief in me. As my daughter once said, you were my lover and my mentor.

"Nothing but death can kill a dreamer"

This is a poignant letter. It's about what might have been, but only in the world of dreams. By the time we met we had made decisions, marriage and children, that should have made the likelihood of love and happiness for us impossible. However, we were two people who were desperately lonely, so we used each other's desperation as our escape route to happiness. But we could only ever have each other, as the pressure of circumstances left the possibility of our having a child in the world of dreams.

"I never want to live without you"

This is a passionate letter. A letter expressing a need that we both shared. It is also a letter about commitment and planning for our future together. We have overcome doubts and obstacles and hope to start living together soon.

"Living without enthusiasm is existing"

There is clearly a tension between your desire to live life enthusiastically and the responsibilities of work, marriage and being a mother. You admit to being "very cynical", then correct that by stating that your cynicism is a form of protection and that "underneath" you are "really innocent and easily hurt". I was able to see your sensitivity, but on occasion your cynicism confused and hurt me. You wrote that what attracted you to me was my "youthful enthusiasm, romance and the desire to do something with my life". The tone of your letter is quite sad. You seem resigned to the mundane and unfulfilling life you are leading. You point out our respective marital responsibilities and state that we must take them seriously. Then you set me "free" by stating, "However, I am sure that this will not be so for you, for if you are determined you can do anything."

"I don't see any horizon to our love, no end to the road, infinity seems a very confining description about the extent of our love"

A letter in which I celebrate what we have found in each other.

"Never let me dominate you or all will be lost"

You list all the things/likes we share, including our similar personalities. "I love you as a person, the mind as well as the body". Then there is an admission: "Remember always, I like you to be stronger, harder even, than me. Never let me dominate you or all will be lost". The letter ends with what I think is the truth of our relationship. "What we have is precious, perhaps only happens once in a lifetime, so let's work to keep it as perfect as we can".

"Jesus was a masochist; God was his excuse"

In a charged and contorted way, I seem to see you as taking the part of God to my Jesus, seeking my destruction by your hands.

The "dreamy girl" and the "wayward dreamer"

I write a sad love letter – "You look much younger, like a dreamy girl." "When will you accept that I love you and will always love you? When I say these things, you brush aside a few strands of my hair and without needing to say anything seem to imply, "We'll see"."

"We have, as you once said, glimpsed a certain kind of Eden"

Time has passed, external pressures have mostly gone, we are married, we love each other and in confirmation of our happiness you write that we made the right decision when we got together. "I still couldn't live without you, just as I couldn't then. I remember the ache when I was without you and the urgency with which I rushed to our meetings. We were made for each other." Using my words you close your letter with, "We have, as you once said, glimpsed a certain kind of Eden."

"With love and gratitude on thirty-five years living together"

You sent me a thank you card for caring for you during your illness. Your words of gratitude are simple, truthful and heartbreaking.

"Just a little thank you"

You sent me an anniversary card, a few months after you had received a terminal diagnosis, in which you write, "I can only hope that the road ahead will yield some relief for us. We still share each other. Long may we do so."

"Hoping for better days"

The message in your last Christmas card to me is brief, "With love and gratitude. Hoping for better days." But the "better days" never came, as you died little more than a month later.

> Life is presence, death is absence. Two statements with an endless distance between them. I sat beside you in the hospice, but you were not there. In losing you, I lost myself. I sat for hours trying to comprehend the finality of your death, that I would never hear your voice, see you smile or hold you again. Without you to come back to, I did not know how to leave. As darkness entered the room, its kindness softened your outline. I left then taking nothing with me but the wound of grief.

"You're my witness, I'm your mutineer"

I love the Warren Zevon song, Mutineer, because it takes me back to us when we first met. I was still young enough to want to show off to you, which given my working-class background, meant trying to impress you with my masculinity. I knew you liked my body, but you, as a middle-class feminist, were ambivalent about demonstrations of masculinity. When I beat a weightlifter at arm wrestling, you seemed only vaguely impressed. You seemed more impressed with my love making, which you described as "lyrical", a description that concerned me, as it didn't seem very masculine.

The hanged mouse

I looked down and felt three things almost simultaneously: shock, sadness and the memory of a medieval image. The netting from a bag had twisted around your throat and had hanged you as you struggled. Although a mouse, you looked strangely human. You looked like The Hanged Man, a Tarot Card depicting self-sacrifice. But does a mouse have a self to sacrifice? You looked peaceful, calm, head resting to one side, eyes shut above nose and comic whiskers. My sadness increased as I removed the makeshift noose. Why had you died? There seemed no rhyme, reason, or fairness to it. An arbitrary end for such a harmless creature. I said no prayer, as I laid you to rest, but my heart was with you.

Buddhists feel compassion for all creatures, because they all share the suffering that is an inevitable part of life, so perhaps I'm an intrinsic Buddhist, or perhaps I'm more compassionate since I lost Christine.

Some are cheated more than others

The ancient Greeks believed in luck and they were a clever people. When I think about Christine, I feel sad for her, because I don't think luck favoured her much. Before I headed off to Kinlochewe, last July, Christine and I assembled a Lutyen's garden bench, which we had just purchased and she had always wanted. I left her sitting on the bench, enjoying a glorious summer's morning, while I drove off. Too soon the bench was put into the garage to protect it from winter's weather and Christine started to develop the symptoms of the cancer that would end her life. Within the last week I have moved the bench (her bench) out of the garage and onto the patio, where she sat on that sunny July morning. Having positioned the bench in the spring sunshine, I thought that Christine had been cheated, given the short time she enjoyed admiring and sitting on her cherished acquisition. That, however, was just one example of where life could have smiled on her more often.

Love is hard, but loss is harder

The Aztecs practiced a ritual that involved flaying a living victim. Metaphorically, the intensity of vehement attack we used, when we argued, amounted to a kind of mutual flaying. What disagreement could have led to such implacable bitterness and bile? After the "war" when we sat emotionally exhausted, desolate and isolated from each other, despite the physical distance between us being insignificant, the cause was obscured by the debris of hate and recrimination. The need to win had resulted in our mutual "destruction". Your tears were external and my tears were internal. After a while someone would speak. Then, gradually, an unspoken truce would develop through tentative, neutral, inoffensive words and observations. Sometimes discussion would take place about the possibility of us going our separate ways. Then we would think about what that implied – never seeing each other again – so we relied on love to heal the wounds. The irony is I know that was the right decision, as your loss confirms every day.

The Maya

My education was abysmal, so I was classed as a failure. I used to quip that I was stupid until I left school. And perhaps you also believed that, because you encouraged me and gave me the confidence that is essential for success. However, I learned that when you fail the first time you spend the rest of your life compensating for your initial failure. My pursuit of knowledge was somewhat idiosyncratic and led me along many strange, interesting paths to various and varied examples of human endeavour and because you loved me and were interested in adventure you travelled with me.

Mesoamerican cultures, e.g. the Maya, Aztecs, Incas (and others), had fascinated me since I read, The Discovery and Conquest of Mexico, by Bernal Diaz del Castillo. Bernal Diaz's first-hand account came from his experience of serving under Hernan Cortez, perhaps the most famous Spanish conquistador.

As you had always wanted to go on a cruise and I hadn't, you came up with the brilliant idea of making it a Caribbean cruise, which included visits to beautiful islands, relaxation on the deck of the ship (for you) and excursions to three Maya sites, Chichen Itza, Xunantunich and Quirigua (for me). Chichen Itza is in the north of the Yucatan Peninsula, in Mexico. It was a large important city for 600 years. At the centre, of Chichen Itza, is the imposing Temple of Kukulcan. I climbed the steps of the temple, while you sat in the sun and read. While climbing I thought about the many victims of human sacrifice whose life would end, horribly, when they reached the temple at the top of the steps. The site of

Xunantunich is in Belize (south of Yucatan), which, when we were there, was beautiful and unspoiled. It is much smaller than Chichen Itza and very near the border with Guatemala. The guide who showed us the site was small and from his distinctive features clearly Maya. He was intrigued by my digital camera, especially after I took his photograph and showed him his smiling face on the screen. The last Maya site we visited, Quirigua, was in Guatemala. Like Xunantunich, it was quite small and deathly quiet. I mention this quietness at the end of a poem I wrote for you:

> "At Quirigua the Maya left silence
> To fill a thousand years
> We add to the silence, which soaks us
> Like sweat on soft cotton –

No words are spoken.

Transience

We appear then disappear, but the continuum is unruffled. This is the essential meaning of our lives, of every human life since man's consciousness deserted the comfort of Mother Nature. The older I get the more closely I watch as people disappear around corners. The fascination is that they are there and then they are gone. Death is turning the last corner.

Death into life

"Sky burial" is practiced by Tibetan Buddhists and involves the dead being exposed to the elements to decompose or be eaten by scavenging animals. Hence, the dead are reduced to their elements, which feed life. Perhaps what we did when we buried your parents' ashes and what I will soon do with your ashes and, hopefully, what someone will do with mine is a form of sky burial, because our elements will merge over time in a landscape that, from a human perspective, is timeless and eternally beautiful.

Your last summer

Summer 2013 must have known that it would be your last summer, as it was the best summer we had had for many years.

A version of the meaning of life

"Life means holding on through the death of dear ones." But how do you do that? What do you hold onto?

Wind chimes

I hate the wind. I hate its blind destructiveness. However, the chaos it brings is redeemed, to some extent, by the sublime sounds it creates from my wind chimes. Sublime the sounds may be, but there is an underlying tonal sadness that makes me think of you.

Our last eye contact

I keep thinking about the night before you died. You were obviously in pain but had not yet relented to accept stronger drugs to give you the relief you needed. When you opened your eyes you looked to the middle distance – you didn't speak. Then you looked at me, but it was difficult to decide if you saw me. Your look was strangely neutral. It made me think that you didn't recognise me (a thought that troubled me and continues to trouble me). I said "hello" and there might have been a movement of your eyebrows that suggested recognition. Your look made me bow my head and cry. I felt like a lost child – your lost child.

Death – the only" awakening"

I finished reading The Snow Leopard recently. I was on an interminable train journey, so the escape to the Crystal Mountain was a much needed, if temporary, Nirvana.

I have read this book many times and I will undoubtedly read it again. No snow leopards were seen (just their footprints), except in the imagination of the book's author, Peter Matthiessen, so his search could be deemed a failure. However, in an existential sense, his journey was a success, as each step brought him closer to the essence of his being as something simultaneously significant and insignificant within the simultaneously changing and unchanging mountain landscapes of the Himalayas. I empathised with this realisation, having felt this sense of existential identity, of belonging, in the Himalayas and other mountain ranges, but, apparently, this was not enough for Peter Matthiessen, because it was still Maya, the illusion of the world of our senses. The Vedas believed that "Maya is Time, the illusion of the ego, the stuff of individual existence, the dream that separates us from a true perception of the whole."

The book describes how he lost his wife, to cancer, before he made the trip to the home of the snow leopard. This was the poignant connection and motivation that led me to read this book again after losing my wife to cancer. However, many years prior to my wife's death, I read the book while trekking in Bhutan knowing that she was waiting for me at home. Then I read it again while plant hunting in Yunnan, knowing that only the pain of emptiness was waiting for me. My wife read The Snow Leopard, but wasn't as taken with the book, or its focus on Buddhism, as I was. Buddhism, which is very much about internal reflection and meditation, made her feel uncomfortable, as she preferred to spend her time on less reflective and measurably more productive and life-affirming pursuits. Recently, I chanced upon a DVD called Milarepa. I bought it immediately, as Milarepa – an 11th century Tibetan Lama – is mentioned and quoted frequently in The Snow Leopard. Initially, Milarepa thought that revenge was the solution to his woes, but as this course of action changed things very little, he decided to follow the path of the Buddha, that is, to renounce the world of Samsara – of human illusions and suffering – to achieve the "awakening" the Buddha had realised.

I wonder if Peter Matthiessen – a Zen Buddhist – achieved some kind of "awakening" before he died, or did he die in a state of existential confusion, which is probably the norm for most human beings? I wonder, as "awakening" involves disentangling your focus from the particular to connect with the universal – the undifferentiated – if it is really achievable and that the actual prerequisite for "awakening" can only be found in death, because death is, assuredly," life" beyond illusion, but is unknowable because of that. Therefore, isn't death the only "awakening" – the only Nirvana?

The Self and other illusions

The Yogic understanding of Self is that the knower Self is identical with the known Self and these are identical with the knower's frame of mind. We think we are integrated beings – that is we are one. We also think we have a Self, but apart from feeling we must have a Self, we have no idea where it is and so we can't prove it exists. However, there are so many words (in common use) with the prefix "self", e.g. self-absorbed, self-centred, self-contained, self-motivated etc, that this would suggest our perception of Self is real. We automatically assume it cannot be part of our organic being, of the nerves, blood and tissue that constitute our body. That would be too messy, not pure enough, not obscure enough. However, despite our squeamishness, about our Self existing in our fleshly bodies, where else can it exist? Perhaps, as a compromise, we might accept the crenellations of our brain – our mental apparatus – as the home of our Self? But if we did, when and how does it manifest itself and in what form? Is it spectral, a ghostlike presence that convinces us we are alive – our own being – and separate from other beings with their own Self? Or is it a homunculus," a hypothetical entity in the mind or nervous system that's used to explain human behaviour or experience." It's as if we have a little person in our brain interacting with us as we live our lives. How does the Self influence the way we react, to suffering and loss for instance? Ultimately, the question arises, do we lead or are we led, i.e. do external experiences influence and direct the actions of our Self, or is there a constant interplay between our internal Self and the influence of external factors?

Essentially, though, are we led by a hypothesis about our minds, which we can't prove, as it reacts to what we experience and then determines our behaviour?

Until your death I thought I was self-possessed, i.e. in control, but after your death my being seemed to disintegrate and, concomitantly, I lost control of my Self. This unravelling began as I sat with your lifeless body. The feeling of having a Self is probably just a comforting and helpful illusion, like convincing yourself you know what God is, or reality is, or meaning is, or knowing is, or being is, when, essentially, you don't know what anything is, except the finality of death that confronts you through the dead person you once loved. Stripped of all illusions, I was just an empty shell sitting in darkness. Eventually, I had to leave you, but before I did, I had to reassemble my battered illusions in my empty shell, so that I could continue to function until my illusions are destroyed by the only reality – death. You had reached the end of your time, but what is time but another human illusion. Change predated time and will postdate humanity. Change had seen you born, live and die, but beyond death change would continue until it had reduced you to the elements that produce life, because the cycle of change proceeds without end. There is no God or heaven, but there is the far more tangible and beautiful process of change within the cycle of life, which is the only salvation available to us.

My days

I live my days as if Christine were still alive. I follow the routines she established. I feel I have to keep doing things in a prescribed way, at prescribed times. I could get in the car tomorrow and head off somewhere/anywhere, but the influence of Christine's routines seems to stop me. Perhaps my fear is that the consolation I get from doing what we always did will disappear when, fully accepting the reality of Christine's death, I break away to confront my "freedom".

Who was Christine?

I suppose it's easy to characterise me – a working-class anomaly with an imagination that took him further than he expected – a loner with a contradictory and fatal flaw, the need to love one person to escape the loneliness. It isn't, however, easy to characterise Christine, as she was a contradictory kaleidoscope of opposing traits. She was warm, cold, generous, resentful, calm, stormy, guarded, open, hurtful, compassionate, subjective, objective, man-loving, man-hating, hopeful, without hope, lustful, chaste, rational, irrational, damaged and damaging. W.B. Yeats wrote, "Never give all the heart, For love will hardly seem worth thinking of To passionate women if it seems certain … An emotionally devastated Yeats's, understandably, advised caution, "For he gave all his heart and lost", I gave all my heart, but, contrary to Yeats's experience, my passionate woman, Christine, reciprocated. But, before she met me, callow, unsophisticated and naïve, for a 28 year old, she had paid "the cost", like Yeats. Hence, when I think of Yeats's poem and I think of Christine, I want to substitute the word men for women in the line, "For love will hardly seem worth thinking of To passionate men if it seems certain". Another factor that made Christine difficult to fathom, in terms of how she would react to things, was her parenting. "They fuck you up, your mum and dad, They may not mean it, but they do". This admittedly well worn, if not threadbare, quote from a Philip Larkin poem was especially true in relation to Christine's emotional responses and feelings of self-doubt. Christine would say I was a changeling, because she couldn't reconcile me with my parents, so I must have come from somewhere, or someone, else. However, if I was a changeling, so was Christine – certainly in emotional terms – as both of her parents personified the chilling austerity of middle-class Protestant Scots, whereas Christine had strong feelings and she wasn't afraid to show them.

What if?

When Christine was 17 she had a boyfriend with whom she was besotted. Her most ardent wish was to marry him, but he was more intent on completing his studies and planning for a future career, so Christine's dream came to nothing. Subsequently, she married, but the marriage was not a success. Then she met me – a rough diamond that needed a lot of polishing and even then, would never shine like her lost love. What if her lost love had agreed to marry Christine? Would they have loved each other enough, had children, been happy? Futile questions perhaps, but it seems worth indulging in a little futility to imagine Christine happy and fulfilled.

Shadows on a beach

You cannot cast a shadow anymore, except one of longing over the rest of my life. But I have a photograph, taken on a beach at Cefalu, where your shadow exists and will persist, as long as I have that image. Your shadow stands next to mine and is, touchingly, recognisable. While I am taking a photograph, you are contemplating Cefalu, which is simultaneously being illuminated by the gradually setting sun and, like a lizard, seems to be absorbing the fading warmth into the fabric of its ancient buildings. In the golden light, Roger II's cathedral – his 12th century gift to world architecture – is the focal point of the photograph my shadow is, apparently, taking. You found my need to contemplate the mosaic of Christ Pantocrator, in the cathedral, a contradictory obsession for an atheist. I tried to explain that while I found the catholic crucifix just a crude accusation, I found the depictions of the orthodox Christ more serene and more inclusive in his, apparent, recognition of humanity's shared suffering.

Photograph 1

A photograph is an image of something, but some photographs convey more than that. When I look at a photograph of you resting your back against a tree, somewhere in Majorca, I recall the smell of an enveloping sweetness and warmth. The memory of that smell confuses the senses, as it feels like a warm embrace, your warm embrace. Your sunglasses, each lens reflecting the sun, rest above your forehead on your hair, which is dappled by the sun filtering through the trees. Sometimes, people say, "If you could look into my heart, you would see that I love you." It's strange that when it comes to love, affection or grief, logically accurate language fails us, so we use words – which although logically inaccurate – better express our feelings. "Smile for the camera", is a throwaway line that probably matches the emotional shallowness of most poses – for most holiday snaps – but not in this photograph. In this photograph your look says, "I'm happy and I love you" and it's coming straight from your heart – how lucky I was!

Photograph 2

In this photograph you look too girlish to be 36. Perhaps it's your short hair that gives that impression, or the open, innocent look on your face. You are wearing a white dress, but I think that was just a coincidence on what was the day of our marriage. You are smiling, but your eyes seem less certain. They seem to be asking questions, questions that suggest uncertainty. "Do you love me?" "Will you look after me?" "Will our love last?" These questions can be read in your eyes. I hope our future together, from the 20th January 1979, answered those questions positively. When I look at this photograph now, I only have one question to ask myself and that is, "How could I not love, look after and commit myself to the person in this photograph?"

Life is a dream

Eastern philosophies, e.g., Buddhism and Taoism, say life is a dream. I think it is a valid metaphor, but at its most valid when your life crosses the threshold from life as a dream to life as a nightmare. To extend the "dream" metaphor, life is a dreamscape that is fraught with potential dangers. These dangers are both external and internal. Perhaps the internal dangers are the most frightening, because they can't be seen and when they are felt they are often ignored. If you are lucky the feeling goes away. If you are unlucky the feeling alters the status of your life from dream to nightmare and then to the non-status of death – where your dream ends and the nightmare for others begins.

"How can I love you if I don't admire you?"

I watched a French film recently and the young couple in it made me think of us when we were like them. They were absolutely consumed by each other. Their love, passion, or lust if you prefer a pejorative biblical term, was all consuming. I have never understood the almost paranoid reactions of some people to physical love, as it is the most selfless, innocent and harmless activity that two people can enjoy. I suppose with religious people it is sinful, because your devotion is to your partner's and your own sexual pleasure, rather than to God. With inhibited people, it must be the loss of control, through the surrender of the body and senses, which is the problem. However, as the quote above suggests, for love and sexual desire to continue, there has to be more than the loss of your "self" and your senses, as they enmesh with the "self" and senses of your partner and that "more" is admiration. I didn't just love and desire Christine, I also admired her and I think she felt the same about me.

Dreams

I have had many dreams since you died, but I can't remember you being in any of them. They have just been the usual rag bag of ludicrous juxtapositions of, mostly indistinct characters appearing, making some kind of bizarre/unlikely contribution and then disappearing. Mostly, I seem to be the onlooker, the done to by events, rather than being in control of events. What is interesting about dreams is the way, from popular songs to ancient philosophy, people have questioned whether life – conscious life – is any more substantial than dream life. Is the only difference that dreams –so called – take place while we are asleep, while the influence of our dreams takes place while we are awake? However, the propensity to live our life in a dream means that we live life as if it will not end, that neither we nor our loved ones will become ill and die. Even when the "dream" is thrown by the nightmare of reality, we continue to live as if in a dream. Therefore, when you died and the dream was broken, I returned to my dream existence as soon as I could to escape the nightmare of reality.

When you are not killing time, time is killing you (1)

When you are bored time hangs heavily on you. Perhaps that's why, almost in resentment, you talk about "killing time". When you are not bored, when you are engaged, happy, heading in the right direction, you never think about killing time, but time is killing you! Life seems to be full of these paradoxes, which defy our capacity to really know how to "play" life. Christine hated boredom. I suppose, in part, that is why she planned everything. That way she avoided the doldrums of having nothing to do to fill up the time or think of ways of killing it. When I consider that we were together for 36 years, I find such a long period of time hard to grasp, as it slipped by so quickly. Perhaps, counterintuitively, we should have worked harder at being bored with each other?

When you are not killing time, time is killing you (2)

I watched you run out of time. I suppose I was running out too, but not as brutally or as literally as you were. Now, I look for ways to use up my time, until my time is used up. Tomorrow evening I'm going to a Yoga class. What will I do with my time there? I think I'm hoping for some kind of release from missing you. However, I'm not hopeful, as I'm more likely to think about you while I'm supposed to be reaching for some kind of physical and spiritual equilibrium. There will be other people there, so that might help, but how can the small talk of strangers ever assuage my need for you?

Morar

These are precious moments. I'm on a beach at Morar. The sand is snow white. The sea is jade green. It is a beautiful May morning. The sun has burned off most of the cloud and there is a static calm that convinces me not to break the spell, but to stand still.

More than a travel writer

I greatly admire an English author who writes travel books. That he writes travel books is true, but his skill as a writer is much greater than that, in fact greater than the skill of most novelists. His powers of description and observation, communicated using highly crafted prose, is truly exceptional. In his travels he has met many different peoples from many different countries, mostly ordinary people with a tale to tell. Of history, his extensive knowledge enables him to speculate about the lives led by peoples and cultures that have long since disappeared. Another skill he has is the ability to engage with the people he meets in an empathic way, which leads them to be open with him in almost heart-breaking detail. Frequently, he becomes like a father confessor to those who have invited him into their homes. Perhaps this happens, because he is a strange foreigner who is just passing through, so they know their confidences will soon fade with their receding memory of the sympathetic stranger. It is a pity Scotland is not exotic enough for my favourite travel writer, as I could easily fulfil the role of a damaged soul in search of the kindness of this gifted stranger.

To die alive, not die dying

I read an article recently, which made a number of points about facing up to death, rather than running away from it. Everybody dies, but nobody wants to talk about it. Some people are almost ashamed of the fact that they are going to die, as the whole process appears so unseemly. In the past, when the doctor pronounced your death sentence you accepted it and started to die. However, things are changing and I think Christine is an example of that change, as she chose to die alive, not die dying.

"And when you're gone you can never come back, when you're out of the blue and into the black"

(Neil Young)

Death is a medical failure, rather than the actual conclusion to life

Doctors, in common with less exalted beings, suffer from this and that, but the one thing they don't suffer from is humility. That is why they view death as a medical failure, rather than a natural conclusion to life. I suppose Christine's doctors were conflicted by her hopeless situation. They had to treat her, but she was clearly going to make them feel uncomfortable, because she was going to die and, in consequence, become a medical failure. I think people, who apply to train to be doctors, should be rejected if they do not understand how important a measure of humility is when dealing with patients and with the inevitability of death as a natural fact, not a vexatious medical failure.

The hopelessness of trying to describe loss

Loss is an absence, something missing, nothing, where before there was something/ someone. We use words to describe things and they function quite well for that. Where words fail, is when they are used to describe an emotional void. Perhaps we should stop clutching at words, which are, fundamentally, incapable of describing loss, as we simply condemn ourselves to stunned failure. Perhaps our tears and the sounds we make when we cry are as close as we can get to describing our loss – albeit incoherently. The sounds of our grief express what words will always fail to articulate.

Company

Sometimes, when I'm in company, I feel lonelier than when I'm alone. I watch the faces, I hear the voices, but all of it just isolates me. What I want then, to release me from the faces, the voices and the isolation, is you, but I can never have you.

Christine's letter

I said at Christine funeral that she didn't do self-pity and the letter she wrote and sent to friends and family, on the 5th of December 2012, demonstrates that. The attack by fate, or the consequences of ageing, or whatever is outlined in a matter-of-fact way, that belies the way our lives and the lives of my mother and father were unravelled by, in my mother's case, dementia and in Christine's case, the diagnosis of the cancer that would end her life. There is a film called, "The Clash of the Titans", which is about Greek myths and mythical characters and the way the manipulative Greek gods, especially Zeus, torture people by allowing them to feel they have achieved safety and then by throwing them into a situation of life-threatening turmoil. Zeus must have read the part, of Christine's letter, where she celebrates the fact that her chemotherapy is working, because that situation wasn't to last.

Tears and asphyxiation

I go to the local hotel to write about us. I'm surrounded by couples who tend to ignore each other. The younger ones seem more interested in their mobile phones than in each other. We are most lucky when we don't even recognise our luck. What I would give to stop writing about you/ us and have you back. I feel like making an announcement, that all the couples in the bar should switch off their mobile phones, cease their sullen reveries and pay attention to each other, hold hands, talk, feel grateful that they have company and, perhaps, are loved. When I leave, the hotel, I feel empty and sad and while driving home I struggle for breath through tears and asphyxiation.

The hills above Glenfinnan

It's taken months for the weather in the northwest to settle enough for me to set off to climb some hills. The forecast isn't wonderful, but it's good enough so I decide to climb the hills on the south and north shores of Loch Sheil, beside the monument to Bonnie Prince Charlie at Glenfinnan. Loud music helps me to get to my destination in a time that would have put you in a state of shock. I suppose I was always the risk taker, in our partnership, while you tried to control my intemperate urges. As I began the long walk to the start of the climb, my intemperate nature was tempered by the grey weather. Where was the sun that was forecast, I enquired of the silent landscape? The answer was supplied by the unchanging grey, which rendered the, potentially, impressive views with a monotone that made me force myself to take a few photographs. Tired of the greyness, I turned inwards and thought of you.

The Roe deer

We were heading for the hospital. You had three weeks to live, but we didn't know that. As is typical with human beings we were still travelling hopefully through life and ignoring how bad things were.

Just before we entered Markinch a Roe deer appeared on the road ahead of us. I slowed the car and put the lights on full beam, so we could watch our graceful pathfinder as she proceeded – almost in slow motion – ahead of us. Although you were in pain, you were intrigued by our silent companion. My impression was that we were mesmerised by this strange occurrence and where/how it would end? The deer's coat was quite ghostly in the car's headlights. Its movements seemed undecided, as it would veer slowly to the right and then to the left. Then after a short distance, but what seemed like a long time, the deer turned left and effortlessly clearing a fence disappeared into the blackness. A Shaman might have said that the deer was a projection of your need and desire to escape your torment. That this delicate, harmless creature was showing you the way back to our ancestral home – the world of Nature. Would that you could have followed her and escaped the pain and futility that lay ahead.

"God"

There was a medic in the hospital where Christine was being treated who was referred to by the nurses – in awe and trepidation – as "God". However, this "deity" was about as much use to Christine, as the one who doesn't answer our prayers. According to Christine, he described her "insides", as "a bit of a mess." However, he pronounced this with that godlike, cavalier arrogance that many medics exude and what could Christine do but listen. While I accept that "the" real God probably doesn't have a conscience, because he is a supreme being, I wonder if the counterfeit gods – the ones in the white coats – think about the impact their attempts at empathy have on the poor patients – their fellow human beings – who are receiving their death sentences in a state of absolute vulnerability?

"Trapped"

Bruce Springsteen covered this Jimmy Cliff song and for a while (a long time) I was obsessed with it. I wonder if you worked out why my listening to this song had become a compulsion. I think not, as it was both selfish and immature and you were neither of these things. The reason I felt trapped was because our more settled and I suppose respectable existence came with the normal range of pressures and commitments, which, I strongly felt, subtracted from us. What I wanted was to be trapped by you, but to be trapped by you when we had more freedom to exclude everything from our world but us.

Self-loathing

There are so many people in the media who love themselves unconditionally. Unconditional love is normally what a mother gives to her child, i.e., a being external to them to whom they gave birth. However, with media people it is their internal child, I presume, that they love unconditionally, as they could never extend that commitment to anything/anyone external to themselves. Such self-centred onanism, expressed in a torrent of ego-burnishing babble, could never countenance, or practice, self-loathing, but it is common enough in Scotland. Christine and I were only children. "An only child is a lonely child", so it is said. I think that is true, but along with the loneliness comes a tendency to be self-critical and to feel a degree (or more) of self-loathing. When Christine was dying, she expressed guilt (a close relative of self-loathing) about the happiness we had sought and found together. "Don't beat yourself up about it" was not available to people like Christine, although she deserved that easy exculpation more than most.

New Zealand 1997

I'm in The Bower Bar, which is a big barn of a pub in Christchurch. I'm drunk and I keep putting money in the Juke Box and I keep playing the same songs. I'm 48 years old and I seem to be having some kind of mid-life crisis. I love the way my cousin's husband, and his mates accept this drunk, crazy Scot, bopping beside the Juke Box. When I crack up, break down, they find a fairly worn looking woman and introduce her to me. As I can hardly focus on her, never mind indulge in some kind of sweet talk, she reads the signs and disappears. My cousin's husband and his mates follow her and leave me to continue with my crisis, which has nothing to do with mid-life and everything to do with missing Christine.

"Whatever's written in your heart"

It was summer, it was hot and we were in the west. I'd torn a muscle in my shoulder and I was sitting in the car recovering when a Gerry Rafferty song came on the radio. I could taste the salt from the tears making their way down my cheeks. I think you thought I was being quiet, because I was in pain. Fortunately, you didn't notice my tears. Why the sadness? Why did I feel, "We'd find a way to say it all someday?" I think it was because of external pressures. We had decided to be, according to accepted custom – morality – immoral. We had left our respective partners and our children for each other. When I think of what we felt for each other and what we withstood to ensure that our love for each other prevailed, the last word that comes to mind is "immoral".

Dealing with it by ignoring it

The more I think about your last few months, the more I try and fail to comprehend what you were thinking about. We seldom spoke about your illness, we just acted as if things would go on as they always had. I dealt with your illness by supporting you. That is, I bought the food you thought you might be able to eat, I prepared it and you ate some of it. Sometimes, your eyes would briefly fill with tears, because you thought I had been kind to you, but how could you think I wouldn't be kind to you? I suppose I just fitted in with how you were feeling. You said, in a letter, that I had the ability to adapt to whatever arose, but was that enough? I was an efficient housekeeper, but perhaps I should have been more than that. I think, because our relationship had been one of equals -physically and intellectually – we didn't know how to deal with the poignancy of your circumstances, so we dealt with it by ignoring it.

Overthinking

Recently I was told that I over-think things. That's probably true, but is it not better to over-think than to under-think? Socrates said, the unexamined life isn't worth living, which seems a more reasonable position than the under-thinker's position, i.e., the unexamined life is much easier on the brain cells. I think, however, this position is an example of the difference between men and women, as Christine also thought I over-thought things. In my own defence, without being an over-thinker I wouldn't be the person I am or be capable of dealing with the numerous challenges and complications life has thrown at me.

Bruch's Adagio from Violin Concerto No 1

Near the start our relationship you played me Bruch's Adagio from Violin Concerto No1. I felt, as I often did in our early days, that we were not going to succeed. That you would go back to respectability and I, simply, would go nowhere. I kept my sense of vulnerability to myself, but the musical phrase, which is hauntingly and heartbreakingly repeated throughout the Adagio, melted my resolve to appear brave and in control of things. My tears, which I could not stop, exposed me for what I was, someone who loved you deeply but was fearful that you might not love me enough, but, subsequently, and over a period of many years you proved me wrong.

"Song of Summer"

I watched a film called Song of Summer, which is about the composer Frederik Delius. To begin with I found comfort in the sadness of the film. I also watched it because we had watched it more than once. Ultimately, however, it did not comfort me, because it portrayed the human dilemma of trying to find meaning in a life ravaged by disease. Delius died from syphilis, which, over a period of thirty years, paralysed him, blinded him and confined him to a wheelchair, but his ability to compose music was unaffected. The film deals with the last five years of his life, when he composed some beautiful music. During this period of his life, a young man called Eric Fenby became Delius's amanuensis. His main task was to transcribe the music Delius had composed in his head. This was a very painstaking process, made more difficult because of Delius's illness and short temper. However, Fenby showed considerable forbearance, because he worshipped Delius and his music. After five years Delius and Fenby had completed their work, so Fenby returned to his home in Yorkshire.

Then Delius's wife, Jelka, became ill, so Fenby was asked to look after Delius, which he did until he died. If Nature and the music it inspired gave meaning to Delius's life, Delius gave meaning to Eric Fenby's life.

Delius's music was influenced and inspired by Nature. He heard in Nature the still sad music of humanity. Although his music embodies his love of Nature, there is always an underlying sense of loss – a recognition, perhaps, that we (unlike Nature) are transient. We might love Nature, but too soon we will have to leave it.

Perhaps, in a way, I was your Eric Fenby, because you gave meaning to my life, but then, when you died, you took it away.

Home is acceptance

We shared this house for many years. It was our house. We lived for each other within these walls. We accepted each other, because we loved each other. Our real home, of course, had little to do with these four walls. Our real home was our acceptance of each other. Now that you have gone, your acceptance has gone with you and although I have this house, I am homeless, because I have lost your acceptance. When the time comes to move on, therefore, it will not be difficult.

Getting used to loneliness – a non-solution

When you lose someone, who filled half of your life and half of the meaning of your life, you carry around your own abyss with you. When your loneliness becomes intolerable you look into the abyss of the person you have lost. You look and you try to find something, but all that exists in an abyss is nothing, so that is all you find. You retreat from the abyss to live your life of routine and loneliness. There is a view that somehow you get used to loneliness and that that is some kind of triumph. That the end point of loneliness is loneliness accepted and that defines your life. I'm glad I did not accept that destiny, turning to life instead. Now the triumph of loneliness and the abyss are far less certain, now I have chosen life again rather than a living death.

Watching your shadow crumple

I left the car, just before 5.30am, to climb An Teallach. Although I rose early the sun had already risen. I was impatient to gain height, so I pushed myself until I was in a long valley, longer than I remembered from thirty years ago, when I first climbed An Teallach. Everything was still. The mountain sighed now and then, or so the light breeze made it seem, but I was the only thing that was moving – following my shadow. The silent world that surrounded me led my thoughts inwards to you. Externally, there was the sound of my boots on the rocks and my silent shadow always ahead – the trick of the sun. Then I watched my shadow crumple, as a sense of hopelessness enveloped me. I watched the shadow lean on its stick and be rocked by my sorrow. Then I sighed, amid the silence, and watched my shadow uncrumple and move on.

"Become what you are, having learned what that is"

This, Delphic, statement, by the Greek poet Pindar (518 BC – 438 BC), is both captivating and confusing – almost two thousand five hundred years after it was written. It assumes there is a definitive "you" i.e., "what you are". It also assumes that it is possible to learn "what that is". If learning what that is were possible, it must involve experiencing and then rejecting things in your life that you feel are somehow intrinsically harmful to discovering and becoming what you are. This also presupposes that you have a lot of control over your life, which is seldom the case. It also assumes that you possess a high degree of intuition, regarding what accords with what you are. I wonder how many people feel they have become what they are and I wonder how many people never learn what that is? In "real" life when the accident of birth has been unkind to you and your main aim is just to get by, you need someone to help you on the road to becoming what you are. It isn't an exaggeration to state that without Christine's intervention and belief in me, my fate would have been very different. That's not to say I have fulfilled Pindar's cryptic instruction, but that's more to do with the impossibility of the task than with any fault in the person I loved and to whom I owed so much.

Imagine a world......

Imagine a world where God had never existed, so people never killed in his name. Imagine a world where love was the first cause and the effect had been to lead people to cherish each other. Imagine the effect that would have had on human history. Millions of people saved from physical death, in the name of God, and millions more from psychological torture, because they had sinned against God. What perversity led people to choose God, rather than love, as their deity? Was it because, while it seemed logical to kill in the name of God, it would be illogical to kill in the name of love? I suppose this would be consistent with the way human beings talk about doing the right thing, while, in practice, usually doing the wrong thing. We confound and condemn ourselves to making the same mistakes, while knowing the solution is (and always has been) staring us in the face – love is all you need. Christine and I were not believers, even when it would have been helpful if we had been, but we loved each other and took care of each other and we never wanted to kill anyone in the name of God.

Christine's ashes

It's been a number of years since Christine and I visited the place where we buried the ashes of her parents. This shows, as I lead my daughter through the trees, which are obviously taller and denser than when I last visited this place. Eventually, we emerge from the trees onto a slope that leads to the little rock face that indicates where Christine's ashes will be buried, close by those of her parents. After burying her ashes, I prepare a place, so that, when the time comes, my ashes can be laid beside Christine's. I look across to the Ardgour Peninsula. I am surrounded by scenery of such beauty that it defies words, of which I speak none. I sit on a rock and sob. I am lost and I know I will always be lost. I also know that the passage of time and the inevitability of change will mean that my ashes will never be with Christine's.

"Care about people's approval and you will be their prisoner"

These are wise words, written by the Chinese philosopher Lao Tzu about 2,500 years ago. These words caution the reader to not care about "people's approval", to avoid being "their prisoner". But I couldn't help wanting your approval, because it validated me and if, in consequence, I was your prisoner I never wanted to be released.

Inverewe Garden

Both of us loved the Northwest of Scotland. The weather could be fickle, but if you were lucky and the sun shone few places – anywhere – could be so breathtakingly beautiful. A favourite destination was Inverewe Garden, which sits beside Loch Ewe and benefits from the warming influence of the Gulf Stream. The garden is full of mature Rhododendrons, Magnolias and Camellias, as well as exotic tree species and an impressive collection of Perennials. When the Rhododendrons are in flower, it is easy to imagine you are walking in the foothills of the Himalayas. The last time we visited the garden was in late summer 2012, just a few months after you had undergone major surgery. I took a photograph of you with your hand resting against a Eucalyptus tree. You were smiling and you looked fit and healthy, but looks are deceiving, as after 18 months had past you were gone and I found myself choosing this photograph for your Funeral Service. I have visited Inverewe Garden several times since your death and each time I touch where your hand rested on the Eucalyptus tree. I know I'm not touching you and I know I can't touch the memory of you, but something compels me to touch the tree and look inwards. I also think of you looking inwards, as, on the same day, I approached the bench where you were sitting. You weren't aware of me, so I didn't disturb your thoughts. Then you looked up and smiled, a smile that barely hid the depth of your sadness. There have been times when strangers have been sitting on that bench, but it is you and your sadness I see, not them.

"He who has a why to live can bear with almost any how"

(Friedrich Nietzsche)

When you were alive you gave my life purpose. When you died that purpose was removed. Your existence underpinned my existence. You were the foundation of my life. When your death removed that foundation my way of living, effectively, collapsed. I am still alive, but not in the way I lived when life was enjoyed, rather than endured, and we gave each other's lives meaning and purpose.

The need to fill the void

It has been some time since you died. When you were here you were all the company I needed. We were together 24hrs a day. Even as you slept, I had your company. I could hold you and feel your warmth, your softness. Now, there is an empty space where you slept. Now, when I lie in bed, I look at that space but never venture there. When you share your life with someone, you talk to them and they reciprocate. The days are filled with each other's company. Since your death there is little talk in this house, because I am on my own. When you are on your own you think rather than talk and thinking, being an internal process, activates other internal processes, like memories you would rather forget. You find yourself moving quietly, which magnifies the silence, which in turn magnifies your loneliness and causes you to break down and, as you must recover or contemplate suicide, you feel even more lost. People are kind when they can fit you in, so you wait for a call, hopefully. You escape to the NW of Scotland, to China – anywhere – and it works for a while, but you are still bound to yourself and the hauntingly empty space once occupied by Christine. It seems, with what there is left of my life, I have two choices, to gradually disappear into a silent mindscape of fragmented memories and live with the consequences or try to escape my loneliness. Christine once said, I was like a force of Nature. If that is true, then I'm turning that force against myself, when what I need to do, in pursuit of life and company that isn't a form of charity, is to seek out fellow travellers and engage with them in an emotionally healthy and life-affirming way. Perhaps then I will be able to think about when I loved Christine, rather than crucify myself because I lost her.

My first holiday without you

Over the years our holiday destinations took us to many mountains and many cities. The mountains were my obsession, while the cities fulfilled your desire for culture. I never gave a thought to the inevitability of our holidays coming to an end but that is what happened, as the things we enjoyed were gradually, but inexorably, nullified by your illness and then by your death.

I'm sitting in Edinburgh Airport waiting for an Amsterdam flight. Thereafter, I fly to Guangzhou, Kunming and, finally, Shangri-La. Normally, you did everything, as far as holiday arrangements were concerned, so this is a new experience for me. I'm also taking a chance, as I have arranged this holiday with someone I have never met before and sent him one third of the cost of the trip. You would never have taken that chance and you would have been concerned for my safety, as a total stranger was about to lead me into the wilds of Yunnan. After 40 hours of flying and waiting in airports, I arrived at Shanri-La, where I was met by my guide the interpreter for the trip. You would have been appalled by the shattering trip to get to Shangri-La, but you would have approved of my Norwegian guide and the Chinese interpreter. You would have thought they were, obviously, nice boys from nice families and proceeded to find out everything about them and given that they would have thought you were a nice Scottish lady, they would have told you what you wanted to know. I was always more reticent with people than you, antisocial you would say, but in the barely three weeks I knew my guide and interpreter we became good friends. This was helped by a shared obsession with my guide and our, we three's, predilection for alcohol after spending long days plant hunting.

Apart from crucifying myself on a hotel bed on my first night in Shangri-La, because I couldn't find a way to accept or escape your loss and crying in a way that scared me, because I felt on the edge of losing control, gradually my time in Yunnan removed me from emotional purgatory through reliable and predictable routine. Routine replaces thought with action, which was exactly what I needed. Days simply followed days in a comfortable and comforting rhythm, of breakfast, driving, looking for plants, photographing plants, residing in different hotels, shaving, showering, eating and drinking. Drinking too much happened regularly and for me the excess of alcohol delivered the Nirvana of avoiding another emotional crucifixion.

I've been home for a week. I never expected the withdrawal symptoms (and not from alcohol consumption) to be so bad. I feel I should have extended my plant hunting trip into every Chinese Province, as an antidote for the loneliness that seeped into my soul the minute I closed my front door.

Transference

I thought about a close friend a lot when I was in China. Sometimes I'd imagine what our first meeting would be like. This consoled me, whether in the loneliness of my hotel room or while walking through the mist and rain looking for plants. Time and thousands of miles passed, then I was home and looking forward to our first meeting. In my mind I had been imagining what would be said, the way we would look at each other, the gentle smiles, the tender embrace and that all would be well. In a way I was repeating the way I behaved with Christine. I would go away, think about Christine, come home and we would remake the emotional bond. But you are not Christine, you are a good friend who is trying to help me avoid emotional disintegration. Logically, I know I should keep my distance from you – emotionally – but no logic beats in a broken heart. You are kind to me, but I misinterpret your kindness, not because I'm stupid, but because I'm lonely. You once said I could be "standoffish" and I know what you mean. Perhaps, for both of our sakes, I should retreat behind that standoffish barrier, at least until I achieve a less vulnerable equilibrium.

Pilgrimage without salvation

For my 50th birthday I went (on my own) to the north of Spain for two weeks. Some people thought that was incredibly indulgent of you and incredibly selfish of me to want, never mind accept, two weeks away from you. But you knew my passion for wild places was integral to who I am, so, yes, you indulged me. I made forays into the remoter areas of the Cantabrian and Asturian mountains, looking for Bears and lilies and although I found a few lilies, I never saw a Bear – not even a pawprint! Now and then I would see signposts for the pilgrimage route to Santiago de Compostela. Many years before my trip to northern Spain, we drove down the length of the Pyrenees. When we got to Lourdes, you asked if we might visit the pilgrimage site. I agreed, but as we mingled with the crowds, we were disturbed by the naked display of need for (I conjectured) cures for illness or salvation or redemption or all three etched on the faces of the pilgrims. While we stood at the entrance to a church, a group (singing what I assumed was a hymn) moved towards us their voices rising in intensity while the look on the faces of the older men, at the front, seemed to combine devotion with entitlement, as they crossed the threshold. It seemed to me they were demonstrating their faith, but they wanted their faith to be rewarded. I was reminded of the words of a medieval heretic, "The heart of man is the church of god, the material church is nothing." You had dallied with Catholicism as a teenager, but even you felt uncomfortable and alienated by this display of seemingly contradictory emotions. Given what I had experienced, in Lourdes, I decided to avoid

Santiago de Compostela and confine my pilgrimage to the mountains, where you can see your deliverance.

Many years later I took your ashes to Glencoe on a journey of pilgrimage without salvation. It was a pilgrimage, because mountains are sacred places to me and I knew you shared my belief. Nobody's death is kind, but your death was especially cruel, so I took you to a place which had fond memories for you. Perhaps being part of a landscape of mountains, forests, rivers and sea lochs, where worship is silent and nothing is demanded because everything you need is given, would bring you some kind of serenity beyond the reach of the living?

Native Primulas

You died about two months before your seventy first birthday. That still seems so unfair to me, not just because I lost you too soon, but because I felt you deserved to live longer. Deserved, however, suggests that life and death are linked to whether you deserve to die, but this way of thinking relates to our Christian past, rather than cold reality. The reality is that we all die, sooner or later, irrespective of whether we deserve it when it happens. Yesterday, I planted some native primulas where I buried your ashes. It was a heartbreakingly beautiful spring day. After planting the flowers, I turned to look around me at the deep blue sea loch and the snow-capped peaks. I knew you were not able to appreciate what lifted and lowered my spirits – in equal measure – the joy of the day and the sadness of it. I also knew that we had in the past stood here together and marvelled silently at such grandeur. I spoke to you and told you about my life now. I also told you I was lost. I don't know why I said that -I still don't. To say you are lost implies that you can be found, but what does that mean? Perhaps grief reveals that you are lost and cannot be found, because being found has no actual meaning. I sobbed, breaking the silence, and then left you, but not before promising to return next spring, when your primulas will be in flower again. I will follow that pattern of pilgrimage until I am unable to reach you and your primulas, whereupon I will visit you in my thoughts until they cease.

Gardening

I have spent more time gardening than I have doing anything else. Such is my interest in gardening that I consider it to be more of an occupation than a pastime. Christine thought I had an obsessive nature and although she enjoyed the garden, she resented the time I spent pursuing my obsession, especially and understandably when she became ill.

I have been tending my garden for over forty years, so long that I feel Nature is now in control. I am simply the observer in half an acre of what is effectively a natural environment, albeit with plants introduced by me. In every month of the year at least one plant flowers. In the depth of winter, a Witch hazel is festooned with spidery yellow scented flowers that last for weeks and glow brilliantly on sunny days. In Spring, the bare ground bursts into colour, first with Snowdrops and Eranthis and then with Hellebores and Crocus, which entice honeybees into their saffron scented flowers. I have watched honeybees collect nectar while enveloped in Crocus flowers and wondered what it must feel like for a small creature to invade the inner sanctum of what, relative to its size, is a large cup-shaped enclosure. Does it feel intimidated, or does its need for food, after a hungry winter, lead it to overcome its fear?

To, apparently, digress, broadly speaking there were two schools of thought in ancient Greece, one that believed in an unseen perfect world, which was inaccessible to human perceptions and one that believed there is nothing beyond what is accessible to human perceptions, i.e. what you see, hear, smell, taste and touch is all there is. Unfortunately, the attraction of "an unseen perfect world" became a focus of Philosophy, the Christian religion and to some extent Science for Millenia. Almost endless permutations of words were deployed in a, failed, attempt to explain abstract concepts like meaning, being, knowing, reality and God. These concepts were understood to be ahistorical, i.e. separate from History and independent of time. A lot of time and wasted effort could have been saved if the evidence before our eyes had guided our thoughts. Fortunately, some Philosophers, during the 19th and 20th centuries, rejected ahistorical reason and replaced it with historical reason, where everything and everyone is part of history.

My history started on the day I was born and will end on the day I die. Then Nature will render me into my elements and through them I will support new life, no afterlife, no God, not needed. My garden also has a history, of which I have been an integral part. It is possible to liberate the abstract concepts, already mentioned, from their unseen, inert world and introduce them to the dynamic world of historical reason. To begin, what meaning does my garden have for me? It has served and continues to serve a fundamental purpose, regarding my thoughts, actions and wellbeing. As for being, I feel a sense of belonging when working in the garden and that what I have created reflects an important part of my existence and belief. The Spanish Philosopher Jose Ortega Y Gasset, who promoted a historical interpretation of man's existence, wrote, "We always live within certain beliefs. (and) With belief man has a feeling of stepping out of himself and into reality." When I step out of myself in the garden, the reality I step into is Nature, which is my God. As for knowing the reality of what I have created in the garden, the evidence before my eyes, especially when the plants break dormancy in Spring, provides confirmation of the miracle I have helped to create. The rebirth continues with the flowering of myriad perennials, shrubs and trees adding to and accelerating the victory of life over the emptiness and darkness of the dead season, winter. I am always transfixed by the return of such beauty, but my feelings will always be tinged with sadness, as it has been some years since Christine left the "magic garden". After she died, I retreated, more and more into the garden, retreating from death into life. I found no meaning in the brutal inexorability of her cancer and my helplessness in the face of her cruel death, so I sought meaning in something I had known for a long time and which I felt was part of me.

Searching for meaning is a need that is natural in human beings. We want to know why? However, there appears to be almost no consensus about what constitutes meaning. We might possess the concept, but we don't know what to say about it. Perhaps, it's not only that we don't know what to say about it, but that we don't have the words with which to say it and that is especially poignant when someone you love dies. However, approximately 2,500 years ago the Greek Philosopher Heraclitus said, "The world is nothing but change."

As I get older, I appreciate the profound simplicity of his observation and the clarity of its meaning. As part of the world, I am – along with everything in Nature – subject to the ongoing process of change. All I need do, to confirm this, is to look at a photograph taken forty years ago and then look in the mirror. The effects of the aging process are obvious and at some point my death and disintegration are guaranteed. I, like Christine, am caught up in the endless cycle of life and death and yet I live my life as if I won't die, despite watching Christine die. For some unaccountable reason I seem to believe that Christine's fate will not also be mine. Perhaps this fiction is necessary to allow me to function. But that is why, fundamentally, life is an illusion and death is the only reality. Perhaps Heraclitus captured this delusion well when he wrote, "Immortal mortals, mortal immortals, living their death and dying their life."

"Stepping from belief into reality

As a human being I have searched for meaning and certainty. Never more so than when Christine died. I read somewhere that a medieval knight had inscribed on his shield, "I am only certain of uncertainty", a sentiment I can relate to. As a non-believer I have never sought meaning or certainty in the concept of the Christian God, as the first cause argument, which contends because the universe exists God must have created it, (one assumes from a vantage point external to the world) is simplistic in the extreme. This isn't surprising, as the biblical explanation is thousands of years old. According to Genesis 1:27 "So God created man in his own image", therefore we know what he looks like – us! However, biblical scholars have insisted that we do not literally look like God. I assume, because that might devalue his significance as an all-powerful deity.

I have often thought that if Native Americans had invented Christianity, there would have been a greater emphasis on the worship of Nature, which would have enhanced and protected our planet. However, the Christian Judaic religions were born in dry, hostile areas, where Nature was either ignored or resented, hence the unwitting complicity of these "unnatural" religions, regarding the destruction of our planet. Nietzsche was raised a Christian then rejected Christianity, because of its fixation on the afterlife, which he thought undermined living and enjoying a natural life and natural instincts. Although what was true in biblical times and is true now, that human beings rely totally on Nature, for clean water, clean air and clean soil (for growing food) to survive, we continue to treat Nature as if it had no intrinsic value. We look to the heavens for paradise, when paradise is all around us. Instead, principally because of the Christian Judaic religions, we live more and more divorced from Nature. If we are extremely rich, we fantasise about fleeing the planet we are destroying to find a planet we haven't yet destroyed. While if we are poor, we pray hard with our eyes closed against the beauty of the world to a God who doesn't exist in a heaven that has never existed in the sky, but could have existed on earth, for relief that never comes. Rich or poor, our perversity in rejecting what can be seen and what supports us (Nature), for what cannot be seen and does not support us (God) is astonishing. Human beings consider themselves to be the most intelligent life form that has ever existed and yet all the signs: over population, climate change, pandemics, famine, the destruction of Nature, war etc., indicate that we will cause our own extinction – and, assuredly, God won't save us.

Throughout my life, I have sought wisdom in Philosophy and other written sources, which has led me to collect fragments of knowledge, rather than answers. These fragments reflect the study of what we mean when we say something exists, when we say we know something and what we mean by reality. Possibly, the reason these fragments contain no definitive answers is because there are none. Perhaps that is because Philosophy has never been able to overcome the conundrum that there must be something before there is something else, i.e. a preceding cause. Possibly, that is why Philosophy could be described as writing about the inexpressible in an inevitably unintelligible way. Given the choice of believing in ahistorical explanations, for God and philosophical concepts like meaning and being etc. – where there is no preceding cause – and an historical explanation, where everything has a preceding cause, because nothing is located outside the world, reality (in the non-metaphysical sense) and my life experiences would lead me to choose an historical explanation.

As for reality (in a metaphysical sense) I think the Roman Emperor, Marcus Aurelius (121 AD – 180 AD) described it convincingly as follows, "The nature of the whole has nothing outside itself. The marvel of its craft is that it sets its own confines and recycles into itself all within them which seems to be decaying, growing old, or losing its use: and then creates a fresh from this same material." Undoubtedly, Marcus Aurelius was able to formulate that description of what constitutes reality, because he lived and thought before Christianity received the Roman imprimatur in 380AD, at the direction of the emperor Theodosius. Without the power of Rome, it is likely that Christianity would have continued as a minor Jewish cult, which, in my view, would have been a blessing for what is now call the Christian world. Earlier Philosophers emphasized the fact that everything in Nature is constantly changing. In the sixth century BC, Heraclitus observed that everything in Nature was in a state of flux – "all things are in process and nothing stays still." While in the fourth century BC, the Chinese Philosopher Chuang Tzu believed that everything in the world transforms into everything else, as everything dies, decomposes and its vital energy is passed on to other things.

To reiterate, a fundamental question that Philosophers and lesser mortals have been asking for thousands of years is, "Does life have meaning?" To answer that question based on an ahistorical perspective requires acceptance that concepts, such as: being/existence, knowing, metaphysics/reality and God are not related to History. They exist without a preceding cause, things in themselves that are beyond human access, but they exert an influence on our thoughts, because we feel life must have a meaning and, for some people, that includes belief in an ahistorical God who created the world – apparently in six days.

Scientists believe the world is a network of events and interactions not ordered in the human concept of time, which is flawed. Our perception of time comprising past, present and future is, apparently, at best a helpful illusion. For instance, if we had no memory we would be confined to *now* (the present) suggesting that time is not independent of humans, but the invention of humans. Until comparatively recently, Philosophy was influenced by the ahistorical views of the ancient Greeks and the assumed existence of the Christian God. Philosophers were frequently abstruse in their philosophizing, which might have been because, essentially, they failed to get to grips with and thereby elucidate clearly their subject matter. The French Philosopher, Henri Bergson, concluded that, "thought is incommensurate with language", that is, they don't match. This disjunction might explain the problem. This opaque impasse was challenged when a Philosophical approach known as Historical Reason was developed, one of its principal advocates being the German Philosopher, Wilhelm Dilthey.

Another proponent of Historical Reason was the Spanish Philosopher, Jose Ortega Y Gasset. Essentially, Historical Reason doubts the idea that things, including the Christian God, can exist without a preceding cause, so everything, therefore, is of this world and exists within the context of History. Ortega Y Gasset rejected Descartes', "I think therefore I am" – where the thinking "I" is of primary importance – and proposes, "I am therefore I think", where living and thinking are conjoined and are essential to conducting our life throughout its history. "Thinking makes human life possible, because it allows man to imagine the future and confront it." "Man has no nature, no fixed or static, or prior nature." In short, man has no nature, but, instead, a history." Our history begins with our birth and ends with our death. We are our own first cause, because as individuals we are unique. No one has ever been us and we have never existed prior to our birth. Therefore, we do not need ahistorical speculations about what preceded us, because, at the individual and historic levels, nothing did. Thinking and acting throughout our lives – our individual history – is all there is. It is the only tale of certainty that is real.

For thirty-six years Christine and I shared our histories. We met and soon the temporary engagement of our histories became permanent. Love and our desire to be together meant we never thought we were being profligate with the time we had. We gave it to each other willingly. In Christine's case she gave me slightly more than half of her time on earth and then she and her history were gone, while I and my history continue. The ahistorical search for being/existence, knowing, metaphysics/reality and God has been and always will be a chimera, because each day you live is all there is until your days – individual history – run out when you die. Human thought, actions and values depend upon specific historical, economic and cultural contexts, so they are not eternal and universal but changing and local. In proposing this, Historical Reason challenged Philosophy as a discipline seeking universal truth, because truth is not universal but contingent upon/ determined by something else.

Final thoughts

While preparing to write my final thoughts about Notes on Loss, I found a photograph of Christine sitting on a beach on the island of Skye. It's summer, it's dusk and the sun is bathing you in soft light. The stillness of the sea suggests it is warm. You sit bare armed and bare footed enjoying the warmth. Your left hand is resting on your head to shield your face from the sun's rays. Your eyes and mouth are smiling at me, as I take the photograph. Perhaps I said something engaging, as your smile and the way you are looking at me makes a connection. What I mean is your smile isn't a pose, it is part of us captured when you were young and to me lovely, which has defied the passage of time and your death, as I can remake that connection every time I look at the photograph. I ask myself, "What is love?". Is it just when the projection of our needs match each other's in intensity? That is, what I need I see in you and what you need you see in me and although over time the intensity of shared feelings will naturally become less, the fundamental connection remains the same. Can I still love you through your image in a photograph taken many years ago? The answer is yes, because the connection is there in your look and that transcends death.

I wrote Notes on Loss, because I was devastated after you died and thinking about you and writing about you gave me some kind of inexplicable hope amongst the debris of hopelessness. I wrote what suggested itself to me, which is why Notes on Loss has no obvious structure. Rather, it emerged out of the chaos of grief. Fragments which were ours. kind memories and cruel memories – also ours. I recall that after a while I took your clothes to a Charity Shop. As I loaded them into the car, I could see you in them, I could see our memories. Something started to happen to me, as I left the shop, something that chilled me and slowed me down, physically and mentally. When I got home, I seemed to move in slow motion until I fell to my knees. I felt I had betrayed you by giving your clothes away too soon, clothes which you loved and chose with great care. I started to cry and then it seemed I could not stop crying, so I feared I was losing control. I started to panic, because I feared I could not find a way of holding on to the equilibrium that was my "self". Until your death, I thought I was self-possessed, but after your death there were times when I felt I was possessed by a "self" whose purpose was to undermine me. Apart from feeling that we must have a "self", I have often wondered why we are so certain of it, as there is no proof that it exists. Essentially, it is a helpful fiction, which is, nonetheless, central to human perception. The integration of my "self", which I had always taken for granted, seemed to be moving towards a harmful disintegration, which was exacerbated by the way my subconscious life seemed to be impacting more negatively – through bizarre dreams and mental images that invaded my mind arbitrarily and chaotically – on my conscious life. More of these attacks occurred, sometimes they were caused by familiar music, sometimes by looking at your photographs, sometimes because of the sheer weight of my loneliness. I felt I was split in two. The external me got up and functioned through each day, while the internal me was my harsh judge who punished me when I did something callous like giving away your clothes. But the interplay between my damaged "self", my subconscious life and my conscious life was less clear cut than cause and effect. It was more as if some unknowable and unreachable cauldron of hurt existed in my "self"/ subconscious mind, which impacted on my conscious mind and conscious emotions without any warning. I found being alone in the house oppressive and vaguely unnerving, so I spent time in a local Bar writing Notes on Loss. I never spoke to anyone and at times I found their chatter intrusive and annoying, but the presence of people in a place that was not my empty house protected me from self-inflicted damage. However, there were times when I could counter the unpredictable impact of my "self"/subconscious mind by looking at our photographs, or a precious video I have of you looking healthy and laughing at me playing the fool. But the most precious thing about the video is hearing your voice. You used to say that you could not remember what your parents' voices sounded like, so I am lucky because not only can I see you, but I can hear your voice and your laughter whenever I want to or need to dispel the sadness of losing you.

I was reading a letter I wrote to you over forty years ago. What astonished me was the freshness and hope expressed through the idealistic words of a young man who was very much in love. The decades that had past had done nothing to diminish the import and impact of those words. I thought people get old, but words don't. They can be almost immortal. Perhaps, I thought, I can bring some of that magic to some of our memories, good and bad, by writing them down in a small book. The one thing that is strangely absent from Notes on Loss is what I owed and still owe you, the confidence to be what I wanted to be, not what other people expected me to be. Pindar said, "Become what you are, having learned what that is". Without your love, guidance and support I would never have achieved the intellectual freedom required to enable me to learn what it is to be myself. My daughter said, "Christine is your lover and your mentor", which was a very astute observation.

The accident of birth placed me in a working-class family. The accident of inheritance gave me my father's imagination. I was loved and cared for and my interest in books and Nature and dreaming were accepted with a smile and comments like, "That's just Alan." I attended what could be described as a proto-sink school, which I left with no qualifications when I was fifteen. I became an apprentice in the Furniture trade. Reading, what interested me, helped me to fill in the gaps in my woefully inadequate secondary education. My imagination and the daydreaming it fostered hadn't deserted me, but it was becoming counterproductive. I would stand, books under my arm, in Edinburgh High Street and feel elated for no obvious reason, other than the transport to somewhere better invented by my imagination – but the tools still waited for me in the workshop on Monday! However, the tools and my application to my trade, practically and theoretically, enabled me to gain a measure of success and, in the words of the old maxim, success breeds success. It seemed to be the case that I was only stupid until I left school. I had also found a more disciplined and productive way of using my imagination, i.e. to imagine succeeding at something and then working towards achieving the imagined objective.

Soon after I became a tradesman and had the requisite vocational qualifications, I found employment as a lecturer, in Furniture Craft, in a Further Education College, which is where I met Christine who was everything I was not. She was older, better educated, more experienced and self-confident. I was definitely not her equal, so, despite the powerful sexual chemistry between us, I was not hopeful that our relationship would last. But it did last, I became her work in progress, her diamond in the rough, which after years of polishing led me to achieve University qualifications. Before she died, she said I had overtaken her, but that was never my intention. My intention was to achieve so she never felt ashamed of me and I think I accomplished that, but only because she loved me and helped me.

I've asked myself the question, what have I learned about Christine's life and death and life and death in general from writing Notes on Loss? I need lived experience, Nature and what I have taken and rejected from Philosophy to answer that question. I imagine a metaphorical room and its "contents". The room is hexagonal in shape, it has a door and a window and is sterile white. In each of the six corners is a human concept, i.e.

Meaning, Being, Knowing, Time, Reality and God. They are self-contained, nothing has preceded them, they do not interact. They are impenetrable to human understanding, because they are beyond our frame of reference, unless you are a believer and substitute faith for evidence, then anything is believable. I open the door and walk across the floor of the empty room to the window. I am aware of the stale odour of ancient Philosophical certainties, which reminds me of the words of Ortega Y Gasset, "Philosophy died a long time ago" and, "Man is a pure and continual doing, a constant activity, is total movement, drawn forward towards a goal." The exact opposite of inert and non-interactive. I open the window to refresh the room and look out to a natural landscape of snow-capped mountains, forests, clear rivers, fields of flowers and a mesmerizing diversity of animals including human beings, all illuminated by the giver of life – the sun. What I see is life, which, inevitably, incorporates, in interactive and interrelated ways, the fundamental processes of change, the gradual decline and death of everything – from the life and death of a mountain to the life and death of a person – and the rebirth of everything from the reordering of that elemental disorder into the continuing diversity of life ad – infinitum.

When I buried Christine's ashes on a hillside in the western Highlands, at the end of what in my mind became the path to the native primulas, I knew her elements would contribute to the process that, ultimately, is the only giver of life on our planet. I sat surrounded by beauty and silence and tried not to think too much about the cruel road she had travelled to this, her final resting place. I still loved her and I knew, as I set in motion Christine's reengagement with life, only my death would end that.

www.ingramcontent.com/pod-product-compliance
Lightning Source LLC
LaVergne TN
LVHW090116080426
835507LV00040B/903